The Rise and Fall of

ANTI-CHRIST

IN THE PROPHECIES OF REVELATION

George E. Vandeman

Pacific Press Publishing Association
Boise, Idaho
Montemorelos, Nuevo Leon, Mexico
Oshawa, Ontario, Canada

Edited by Ken McFarland
Cover by Tim Larson
Cover Photo by Comstock / Photofile
Type set in 10/12 Century Schoolbook

ISBN 0-8163-0634-6

86 • 87 • 88 • 89 • 5 • 4 • 3 • 2 • 1

Contents

The Year 2000

Come with me to the year 2000. It's not so far away, you know. What will life be like in the twenty-first century?

Picture the place where you will work. Imagine the futuristic vehicle you will own—maybe your personal space shuttle! And fancy the exotic new food to tempt your taste buds. Will there be enough to feed us all?

Will our cities be centers of commerce and culture—or playgrounds of rats and gangs? Will we enjoy peace on earth—or suffer the horrors of doomsday?

We are brimming with curiosity about the future. But, even more, we crave security. We *need* to know what's ahead for us and our loved ones. And we *can* know more than you may think.

Will Jesus return to earth by the year 2000? Many believe He will. Others wonder whether nuclear war will erase the human race first. How can we know what's waiting around the corner? Who can we trust to guide us into the future?

Whenever my wife Nellie and I shop for groceries, we see the colorful tabloids at the checkout counters. You've seen them too. Sometimes the supermarket psychics offer us bold, new predictions. Often they simply recycle the same headlines from the year before. Many disappointed readers have learned not to put faith in their forecasts.

We get more trustworthy information from God in the Bible. Knowing the end from the beginning, our heavenly Father has unfolded our future in the prophecies of Revelation. This last of

Scripture's sixty-six books was recorded about 96 A.D. by the apostle John while exiled on the remote island of Patmos. It's full of exciting and essential information for us today.

Would you like to discover God's plan for this planet? Then join me as we explore Revelation's fascinating forecasts. Perhaps you've been avoiding Revelation. Many Christians recoil in fear from its beasts and dragons, hailstorms and earthquakes. But there's no reason to be afraid.

I am reminded of that dark and stormy night long ago when Jesus walked on water. Picture the scene. While gale-force winds roar at the frightened disciples, the raging Sea of Galilee threatens to swallow them alive. Now a ghostlike figure appears. And it's moving toward them! Their fear becomes heart-pounding panic. Just when their doom seems sealed, the floating phantom speaks with the Master's comforting voice: "It is I; be not afraid." The storm is stilled.

What an experience! The object of terror turned out to be a revelation of Jesus, their friend. This is what we find with the book of Revelation. All anxiety vanishes when we read its opening words in chapter 1, verse 1.

"The Revelation of Jesus Christ, which God gave Him to show His servants—things which must shortly take place."

You can now see why we need not fear the book of Revelation. It simply reveals the Lord Jesus Christ and His blueprint for our future. Our time invested in this book will be richly rewarded. Look at verse 3: "Blessed is he who reads and those who hear the words of this prophecy, and keep those things which are written in it; for the time is near."

Would you like to claim these special benefits reserved for you in studying this book? Then let's get started right now. First I'll introduce you to Revelation and explain the secrets of decoding its symbols. Let's read verses 5 and 6: "From Jesus Christ, the faithful witness, the firstborn from the dead, and the ruler over the kings of the earth. To Him who loved us and washed us from our sins in His own blood, and has made us kings and priests to His God and Father, to Him be glory and dominion forever and ever. Amen."

Here we see Jesus presented as our Saviour, risen from His

death for our sins. How comforting to find the blood of Christ right here in this book which is famous for its beasts. This is the same gospel of salvation so near and dear to every Christian—Jesus the Lamb of God.

A number of years ago a lighthouse was being built on the rockbound coast of Wales. With the building nearly completed, legend has it, one of the workmen stumbled and fell back through the scaffolding to the rocks below.

The other workmen, shocked at what had taken place, didn't dare look down for fear of being unnerved by the sight. Heavyhearted, they backed down the ladders, but to their surprise and happy relief, saw their fellow workman lying upon a mound of grass, shaken and shocked. Bruised, to be sure, but not seriously harmed. Beside him lay a dead lamb. A flock of sheep had been wandering by, and a lamb had broken his fall.

A Lamb broke your fall! A Lamb broke mine—the Lamb of God that takes away the sin of the world! This is the revelation of Jesus we find in the last book of the Bible.

However, Jesus offers the lost human race more than salvation from sin and membership in heaven's royal family. He also rules the kings of the earth. Because He pilots this planet, we're not left to the mercy of governments and terrorists. We need not fear their threats or bombs. Bad things will continue to happen to both good and bad alike. We are living in the midst of a controversy—a conflict between Christ and His enemy, Satan. But friend, nothing happens down here without our Lord's permission. As the song goes, "He's got the whole world in His hands" in spite of its potential for trouble. That's welcome news, isn't it?

Revelation also proclaims the Lord Jesus Christ as the soon-coming King of glory. Notice verse 7, still in the first chapter: "Behold, He is coming with clouds, and every eye will see Him, and they also who pierced Him. And all the tribes of the earth will mourn because of Him. Even so, Amen."

The second coming of Jesus is the great climax of all the books of the Bible. Especially Revelation, which explains through its prophecies what's in store for us before Christ's return.

Before we decode the symbols of this book, let's learn a lesson from Pearl Harbor. Who could ever forget that December day when Japanese bombers swooped from the sky and swept us into World War II? America was caught completely by surprise. But it didn't have to happen that way. You see, United States intelligence had cracked the secret Japanese code. Daily we intercepted messages about an ominous and imminent offensive in the Pacific theater. Yet, incredible as it may seem, nothing much was done to prepare Pearl Harbor for the impending attack. America was asleep that fateful Sunday morning.

We had cracked the code. But we didn't heed the warning. What a shame!

But the United States learned its lesson. We finally put to practice information gained from breaking the code. Six months after Pearl Harbor came the dramatic turning-point, the Battle of Midway. From secret intelligence received through decoding, American pilots knew the precise location of the vulnerable Japanese carriers. With that crucial information we reversed the trend of defeat and went on to win the war.

You can see the lesson for us today. Decoding symbols won't prepare us for the battle ahead. Not unless we put into practice what we discover in the decoded message. We could become expert Bible scholars, yet be lost for not applying what we learn about Christ and His truth.

Are you with me? Now let's find out how to decode these symbols of prophecy. First we must realize that personal opinions, however interesting they may be, contribute nothing to our study. Peter the apostle tells us that no Scripture is open to private interpretation. We only confuse ourselves when we bring our own baggage into the study of the Word. How much better to accept what God offers and follow where He leads.

We learn so much from children! A friend of mine has a little boy named Stevie, who loves to go places with him. Anyplace at all, it matters not where, just so long as he can be with Daddy. Whenever Stevie sees his father heading for the door, car keys in hand, he pleads, "May I go with you?" Only after they start on their way does he ask, "Daddy, where are we going?"

Are we willing to trust our heavenly Father and go anywhere

the Bible leads us? Then we're prepared to decode the prophecies of Revelation.

Just how do we mine the treasures of God's Word? By comparing scripture with scripture. One text unlocks the meaning of another. And since all sixty-six books are linked together, we need to search the whole Bible to understand Revelation.

Now shall we go for a test drive? We hear so much about the beasts of Revelation. What does a beast in prophecy mean?

To decode this symbol we'll visit the book of Daniel. We find special help here in Daniel for understanding Revelation. That is because this book is the Old Testament companion of Revelation, sharing many of the same symbols. Let's read chapter 7, verse 23: "Thus He said: 'The fourth beast shall be a fourth kingdom on earth.' "

So beasts represent kingdoms, or nations. We use the same symbolism in our world today. For example, you know that the United States is symbolized by an eagle. England by a lion. Russia is pictured by a bear. And so on.

Do you see how much satisfaction there can be for you in decoding prophecy? It's simply a matter of probing the Bible to find explanations of its symbols. Simple enough, wouldn't you say?

Let's proceed with our study. Maybe you've noticed that most of the beasts—the nations—of Bible prophecy emerge from water. What then could the symbol of water represent? "And he said to me, 'The waters which you saw, where the harlot sits, are peoples, multitudes, nations, and tongues.' " Revelation 17:15.

There you have the answer. Water means people—multitudes of people. Once again a Bible symbol is echoed in our everyday language. You've heard the expression "a sea of faces." Large crowds of people are described as an ocean. So beasts emerging from the sea represent nations arising from an area of crowded population.

With one important exception, the beasts of Revelation come from the sea—that is, they originate among the crowded countries of the Old World. Let's learn about this special nation in the famous "mark of the beast" chapter, Revelation 13. After reading the description of this unique beast in verse 11, we can decode its meaning. "I saw another beast coming up out of the earth, and he had two horns like a lamb and spoke like a dragon."

What nation does this beast represent? Well, let's fit the pieces of the puzzle together. First, the time setting. This new nation is involved with the final mark-of-the-beast struggle immediately before the coming of Christ, so it's obviously a last-day power. A relatively new nation.

Why does this country arise out of the earth rather than the sea? We learned that water represents an area of many people, so earth would symbolize a new territory away from the crowded Old World of Europe and Asia. Just as soil contains some water, but not much, the nation springs up where there are some people—a few scattered natives, perhaps. We have a new country born on a new continent.

This nation differs from already established powers in another way. Instead of wearing crowns on its horns, like other beasts, it has two horns without crowns. So this New World nation without a crown is not a kingdom. There is no royalty to rule by force. We have here a new form of government. Could this New World republic be the United States?

There are some striking indications. Even the description of a beast with horns like a lamb reminds us of the American buffalo. What do these lamblike horns represent? Christ, of course, is referred to as the Lamb. What was His idea of government? "Render to Caesar the things that are Caesar's, and to God the things that are God's." Mark 12:17. This calls for clear distinction between the government and the church.

In the Old World, church and state formed a unit. Sometimes the government controlled the church. Often it was the other way around—the church ran the government. But America is different. The first amendment forbids Congress from interfering with religion, in order to be fair to everyone. In order to be free.

Now notice something else about our New World republic. Revelation 13 describes its power to lead the whole world. The United States is the most influential nation on earth. What a responsibility!

Unfortunately, the Revelation indicates that America will take some unexpected turns in the near future. The lamblike nation reverses its gentle manners and behaves like a dragon. Evidently some unusual and distressing events will soon occur in America.

What is going to happen? We'll decode the future of the United States in the seventh chapter of this series, "Bloodstained Stars and Stripes." Don't miss that vital study.

Whatever may be waiting for us between now and the year 2000, thank God we don't have to worry about it. Our world may seem out of control, but it's not. God controls our destiny. However confusing and discouraging the outlook may be, remember He will protect His children and fulfill His gracious purpose for our planet.

And the same God who guides this world can bring harmony to your life. No problem of yours is too big for Him to handle. He sustains the stars. And nothing that disturbs your peace is too small for Him to notice, for He organized the tiny atom.

Are you struggling to save your marriage? There's hope and help in Jesus. Have finances forsaken you? Are you hounded by pain or guilt or loneliness? Take heart. Our Father in heaven loves you dearly. Jesus can meet your every need.

But the Saviour won't force Himself on you. He patiently waits for you to ask Him into your life. Here's His gracious invitation: Revelation 3:20. "Behold, I stand at the door and knock. If anyone hears My voice and opens the door, I will come in to him and dine with him, and he with Me."

How much the Saviour enjoys this fellowship with us. Just as we cherish the companionship of our loved ones. The story is told of a little girl from the city visiting Grandma's farm. After a wonderful morning riding horses, they enjoyed a picnic lunch by the river. Then they explored the woods behind the farmhouse. Following supper, they cuddled for stories beside the crackling fireplace. All too soon it was time for bed. As Grandma tucked the yawning girl under the covers, a sudden crash of thunder jolted them both.

"Grandma!" cried the child. "I'm scared! Can I sleep with you?"

Of course, Grandma was delighted to carry the little darling to her room in the darkness. As they settled off to sleep, one last question came. "Grandma, is your face turned toward me?" Assured that it was, the little one found rest at last.

Friend, as the thunders of final crisis roll across our land, we need not be afraid. The book of Revelation assures us Jesus is with us. And His face is always turned toward us.

The Day After Doomsday

You've just finished dinner in your favorite restaurant. Relaxed and refreshed, you rise from the table and head for the coat rack. As you button up against the cold, the wail of an air-raid siren sends a shiver up your spine. "That's strange," you wonder. "What an unusual time to test the Civil Defense System."

Stepping outside, you notice police cars racing by, lights flashing. Helicopters are whirling overhead. Men are shouting—women screaming. What in the world could be happening?

This is no test. This is doomsday.

It has already been twenty minutes since hundreds of missiles roared out of their distant silos. This moment, those demons of death are streaking over the Arctic Circle toward our beautiful and spacious skies.

Fifteen minutes more. That's all we've got left. "Oh God!" somebody screams, "what do we do!" Hell from the clear, blue sky. Everything we own and everyone we love vaporized in a flash. Nothing but ruins and ashes left for the day after.

Could it really happen? We don't like to think about it. I'm not trying to frighten anybody—you know me better than that! But everybody seems to wonder whether our world might be wiped out by nuclear war. What do the Scriptures say? Let's find out. We need to get some background information first; then we will spend the rest of our time in Revelation. I think you'll be delighted as we discover what God has in store for His people. "The day of the Lord will come as a thief in the night, in which the heavens will pass away with a great noise, and the elements will melt with fervent heat; both the earth and the works that are in it will be burned up." "Nevertheless we, according to His promise, look for new heavens and a new earth in which righteousness dwells." 2 Peter 3:10, 13.

No question about it—doomsday is on the way. A destruction of this earth by fire. Not by nuclear warheads from man, but by the day of the Lord. Is this bad news? Not for God's committed people. The day after will open the door to happiness ever after for God's people.

Unfortunately for unbelievers, this day of the Lord will be an unexpected surprise. Their pursuit of business and pleasure will be shattered by the sudden destruction of this planet. Doomsday will come as unexpectedly as a thief in the night, the Bible says. And this despite a worldwide warning! On September 21, 1938, a hurricane of monstrous proportions struck the East Coast of the United States. William Manchester, writing about it in his book, *The Glory and the Dream,* says that "the great wall of brine struck the beach between Babylon and Patchogue [Long Island, New York] at 2:30 p.m. So mighty was the power of that first storm wave that its impact registered on a seismograph in Sitka, Alaska, while the spray, carried northward at well over a hundred miles an hour, whitened windows in Montpelier, Vermont.

"As the torrential forty-foot wave approached, some Long Islanders jumped into cars and raced inland. No one knows precisely how many lost that race for their lives, but the survivors later estimated that they had to keep the speedometer over 50 mph all the way."

For some reason the meteorologists—who should have known what was coming and should have warned the public—seemed strangely blind to the impending disaster. Either they ignored their instruments or simply couldn't believe what they read. And, of course, if the forecasters were blind, the public was too.

"Among the striking stories which later came to light," says Manchester, "was the experience of a Long Islander who had bought a barometer a few days earlier in a New York store. It arrived in the morning post September 21, and to his annoyance the needle pointed below 29, where the dial read 'Hurricanes and Tornadoes.' He shook it and banged it against the wall; the needle wouldn't budge. Indignant, he repacked it, drove to the post office, and mailed it back. While he was gone, his house blew away."

That's the way we are. If we can't cope with the forecast, we blame the barometer. Or ignore it. Or throw it away!

Only once in history has a worldwide storm warning been issued. The forecaster was Noah. God Himself had told him to warn the world of a global flood. And Noah showed his own faith in the forecast by beginning at once to build a huge ship in which all who believed the warning could escape.

But human nature was exactly what it is now. The people laughed at Noah, called him a fanatic, a man deranged, made his boat a tourist attraction—and were caught by surprise! History will repeat in our day as we near the end of the world.

Since Christ will come unexpectedly, does that mean the world will be without warning? Not according to the apostle Paul.

Remember Pearl Harbor? The Japanese surprised us even though we had advance warning of their attack. But when those bombers swept down from the sky, we certainly knew they had arrived.

That's how it will be at the return of Jesus. Despite worldwide warnings, the unsaved will be surprised. But the Bible says every eye will see Christ coming. See Revelation 1:7. Every living soul on earth will be watching. Let's read Paul's description of Christ's return in 1 Thessalonians 4:16, 17, "For the Lord Himself will descend from heaven with a shout, with the voice of the archangel, and with the trumpet of God. And the dead in Christ will rise first. Then we who are alive and remain shall be caught up together with them in the clouds to meet the Lord in the air. And thus we shall always be with the Lord." Imagine what it will be like to hear Jesus shout for joy as He descends from heaven. And to hear the mighty trumpet of God. Christ's coming will be the most vocal, the most spectacular event of all time. And not a soul will miss it!

Picture the glorious scene if you can. The Son of God piercing the vaulted heavens, moving down the star-studded highway of the skies, attended by myriads of angels. Then He calls out with a voice of thunder, "Awake, you that sleep in the dust of the earth! Arise to everlasting life!"

And loved ones you have lost will hear. That voice calling the dead will be heard the world around. Families will be united. Children snatched away by death will be placed again in their mothers' arms. What a reunion day!

As the resurrected saints are drawn upward to meet Jesus, we who are alive join them in the air. Imagine the feeling! Defying gravity, we soar through the sky. Without a spacesuit, we sail past the stars up to our heavenly home. What a reunion day! What a homecoming we'll enjoy when Jesus comes! What awaits us when we pass through heaven's pearly gates? Let's read our Lord's familiar promise. You probably know it by heart.

"Let not your heart be troubled; you believe in God, believe also in Me. In My Father's house are many mansions; if it were not so, I would have told you. I go to prepare a place for you. And if I go and prepare a place for you, I will come again and receive you unto Myself; that where I am, there you may be also." John 14:1-3.

And what a welcome that will be! Angels crowding about us, singing songs of joyous praise! A homecoming banquet to surpass any dinner we've ever enjoyed on earth! And, best of all, the Father Himself will introduce us to our paradise home.

And what a home it will be—heavenly mansions! What will they be like? Certainly more glorious than the richest dwellings on earth. Even more breathtaking than Hearst Castle!

Come with me up the beautiful California coast to the village of San Simeon. Set back from the beach in the hills lies the most magnificent building in North America. It is the secluded castle built in the 1920s by the famed publisher, William Randolph Hearst.

Let's pretend it is yesteryear, and we have been invited by

Mr. Hearst to join him for dinner at his mansion. As we round the corner of La Cuesta Encantada—The Enchanted Hill—we catch our breath. Just look at those magnificent gardens, spacious pools, and exquisite statues! See the rambling walks adorned with fountains of fantasy and flowers of every color. And below us in the valley, exotic animals frolic in the world's largest private zoo.

Now we approach the castle itself with its thirty-eight bedrooms, fourteen sitting rooms and thirty-one bathrooms—100 rooms in all. And if that's not enough to impress you, the three adjacent guest houses boast an additional forty-six rooms.

Greeting us warmly, Mr. Hearst shows us around. First we go to the library, with its 5,000 rare books and fabulous collection of antique pottery. Next we pass to the game room, with its rare Gothic tapestry and antique Persian tiles. Then on to the private cinema. Mr. Hearst explains that many of the walls and ceilings surrounding us once graced the grand palaces of Europe.

But we must not linger. Dinner is ready. Entering the dining hall with its huge, crackling fireplace, we take our seats at 300-year-old monastery tables underneath silk banners from Italy. What a meal!

And what an evening! Finally our visit draws to a close at the incredible Roman pool. We gasp at the stunning sight of alabaster lamplight reflected in the water from thousands of eighteen-carat gold tiles.

Our visit over, we bid goodbye to Mr. Hearst and get back to daily living. But not for long. Jesus is coming soon to take us home to mansions far more glorious than any palace on earth!

One astonished guest at San Simeon remarked that it would take, not weeks or months, but perhaps years to examine all the treasures hoarded at the castle. And Hearst wasn't even finished! After three decades of work, he died with his pet project incomplete. And someday soon that beautiful castle, along with everything else on earth, will be destroyed by fire at the coming of the Lord Jesus Christ. But our mansions in heaven's Holy City will stand forever.

Here in Revelation 20 we'll learn more about God's wonderful plan for our future: "Blessed and holy is he who has part in the first resurrection. Over such the second death has no power, but they shall be priests of God and of Christ, and shall reign with Him a thousand years." Verse 6.

The raising of believers when Christ comes is called the first resurrection. At a second resurrection, those who rejected Jesus will face judgment and second death. We will learn about that in the next chapter.

So we will spend our first thousand years reigning with Christ in heaven. You know the beatitude, "Blessed are the poor in spirit, for theirs is the kingdom of heaven." Matthew 5:3. But Jesus also promised, "Blessed are the meek, for they shall inherit the earth." Matthew 5:5. Not this planet as we know it. A new earth, pure and unpolluted, redeemed from the ravages of sin, sickness, and death.

How will we take possession of this earth made new? Believe it or not, following our thousand years in heaven, we will move with the Holy City to earth. This is so incredible! I could not believe it if I had not seen it in the Bible. "And I saw a new heaven and a new earth, for the first heaven and the first earth had passed away. Also there was no more sea. Then I, John, saw the holy city, New Jerusalem, coming down out of heaven from God, prepared as a bride adorned for her husband. And I heard a loud voice from heaven saying, 'Behold, the tabernacle of God is with men, and He will dwell with them, and they shall be His people, and God Himself will be with them and be their God.' " Revelation 21:1-3.

Can you imagine what it will be like to move with the Holy City from heaven to earth? According to the Old Testament prophet Zechariah, Christ will stand that day upon the Mount of Olives, just outside the ruins of present Jerusalem. His feet will divide the mountain into a great plain on which the New Jerusalem will rest. And earth will be created anew before our very eyes!

Why would God move the capital city of the universe from heaven to our lowly planet? Simply because we are His special people. God so loved the world that He *gave* His beloved Son to this world. Jesus was not a loan but a gift. And He still belongs to us today. Forever our Saviour will be one of the human family, our brother as well as our Lord! The scripture we just read said, He "Himself will be with them and be their God." Remember?

And Jerusalem, where Jesus suffered and died for our sins, will be the place of God's eternal throne. Throughout ceaseless ages the citizens of the universe will worship with us at the site of our salvation.

We learn more about our new earth in Revelation 21: "And God will wipe away every tear from their eyes; there shall be no more death, nor sorrow, nor crying; and there shall be no more pain, for the former things have passed away. Then He who sat on the throne said, 'Behold, I make all things new.' " Verses 4, 5.

No more death! No more crying! No more pain! Goodbye arthritis and brain tumors! Farewell loneliness and disappointments! All things new with Jesus!

And there is more to explore about our eternal inheritance in the coming chapters. Meanwhile, remember that God will preserve our planet till the day of Christ's return. He will spare us from destroying ourselves by a global nuclear holocaust. Of course, it's possible some of our cities will be wiped out by warheads. We have already had Hiroshima and Nagasaki, you know. But Jesus said this world's buying and selling, building and planting, marrying and giving in marriage will continue uninterrupted until He breaks through the eastern sky.

I propose no political solution for the nuclear dilemma. Suppose the superpowers disarm all their warheads. That would be wonderful indeed! But it would hardly resolve the nuclear threat. Over twenty nations right now have nuclear capabilities. Some of them already have the bomb.

We have come to the point where positive thinking is irrational. What happens when terrorists flex muscles of megatons? A ten-kiloton device—just three kilotons less than the bomb that leveled Hiroshima—can fit inside a medium-size car. Can you imagine what one madman could do to Washington, D.C.? Sooner or later such a holocaust will happen—unless God intervenes.

No human cure exists for the troubles of this world. Instead, I point you to the promise of our Lord and Saviour—Jesus Christ: "I will come again."

Think about the glorious day of Christ's return. Think about it over and over. Let it give you something to live for. Could anything be more exciting to contemplate?

Seeing first a small, black cloud in the eastern sky. Watching it move nearer and nearer till it becomes a glorious white cloud. A cloud like none you've ever seen before. A cloud of angels— uncounted angels. Hearing a sound like none you have ever heard before. The sound of a trumpet echoing 'round the world. A voice like none you've heard before. The voice of the Lord Jesus calling the dead to life. The earth shaking. The tombs bursting open. Angels everywhere carrying little children from broken tombs to their mother's arms. Shouts of joy as loved ones long separated by death are reunited, never to part again!

And then, together with those resurrected ones, we who have waited through the long night are caught up into that angel starship, ready for the trip home.

I like to picture that space vehicle. A cloud of shining angels. A cloud chariot with living wings on either side. A rainbow above it and the appearance of fire beneath. Jesus riding the cloud—and not a person missed who really wanted to make the trip. Ten thousand angels surrounding the cloud and singing the praise of their Creator. Moving past the stars. A living starship on the way to the City of God!

I want to be there, don't you?

Meanwhile, God will take good care of us. So what if trouble and pain and disaster crowd our days and interrupt our nights? What if the wail of the siren is always with us—the whine of missiles, the roar of bombers, the thunder of approaching storms?

Let these simply remind us we have a better place to be and an absolutely fascinating way to get there. The great airlift, not by space shuttle, but by cloud to the city of our God!

Will your name be on the passenger list? It can be. There's only one requirement. It's the word *pardon,* written in the blood of the Lord Jesus Christ, beside your name. I urge you to permit Him to make your reservation today.

Hitler's Last Gasp

Auschwitz—Dachau—Ravensbrook—Nazi death camps.

Without a doubt the horror of modern history is the Holocaust. Hitler's massacre of innocent millions still staggers our understanding. Like smoke hovering over a furnace, unanswered questions linger on to haunt us. How did Hitler develop such gluttony for brutality? And what will God do to punish him?

Imagine, if you will, God asking your advice on judgment day. He wants you to help Him in deciding how to punish sinners. As you stand beside the great white throne, a man named Tom steps up to be judged. Years ago he discovered his wife at a motel hideaway with another lover. In a fit of jealous rage, Tom shot them both. One rash act. Otherwise, he lived a decent life. What sentence should Tom receive?

Next comes Karen, a shy teenager. Trembling in fear and shame, she tearfully admits to shoplifting a camera from K-Mart. How long should Karen suffer for her sin?

And now you meet that mastermind of mass extermination, Hitler himself. Little question that this monster of more than six million murders deserves to burn in hell. For a long time. A year maybe? Perhaps a thousand years?

Suppose God wants Hitler to burn forever for his incredible atrocities. You might understand that. But what if God also condemns Tom and Karen to suffer Hitler's fate? Sentencing all three to share eternity in the fire. No concern for their differing degrees of guilt. Does that sound fair?

Yet many teach that all sinners suffer the same sentence. That all burn in the flames of hell as long as time shall last. Forever and ever and ever. And that's not all. They believe God has been sending people to hell for thousands of years—beginning with Cain, who long ago killed his brother. Consider this. If Hitler went to hell when he died, even if he burns forever, he would still escape many centuries of the pain that Cain already suffered. Would that be just?

Would God punish sinners for centuries, only to call them up on judgment day to see whether they are really guilty? Tell me, friend, what kind of God do we have? Something is wrong here, wouldn't you say?

What's going on? Satan wants to make us hate our heavenly Father. So he twists the truth about God's love.

Let me read something written years ago. It may shock you."The sinner lies chained down on a bed of red-hot blazing fire. . . . The fire burns through every bone and every muscle, every nerve is trembling and quivering with the sharp fire. The fire rages inside the skull, it shoots out through the eyes, it roars in the throat as it roars up a chimney. So will mortal sin be punished . . . forever and ever!"

Believe it or not, this particular description of hell was published for the benefit of children. To make them respect God. "Incredible!" you gasp. Yes, indeed. God has been pictured as more savage than the worst terrorist—more cruel than the most bloodthirsty dictator!

Small wonder thousands have become unbelievers. They cannot connect the existence of a loving God with divine lust for endless torment. Robert Ingersoll, for example, might have become prince of preachers instead of foremost of infidels. But one day as a boy of ten he went with his father to hear a sermon on hell. The minister's demented descriptions incensed the lad. As young Ingersoll left the church, he turned and glared at his father. "If this is the kind of God we worship," the boy said between clenched teeth, "I want no part of Him. I hate Him!" Ingersoll's young heart could not handle such injustice. So that gifted intellect plunged over the cliff into unbelief.

Many today spurn such a revolting concept of God's wrath.

Only about half of Americans believe in a burning hell. Just 5 percent surveyed by the *Des Moines Register* and *Tribune* think they are headed for hellfire themselves. Of course, 31 percent are sure they know someone else is going to hell!

What does Scripture say about the fire? Once again we will probe the secrets of the Bible's last book. But first we must build a framework from other portions of God's Word.

In our last chapter, you may recall, we learned that those who die believing in Jesus will be resurrected at His coming. Then all of God's people travel together up to heaven to reign with Jesus for a thousand years.

Now we will study the future of those found unprepared when Jesus comes. "As it was in the days of Noah, so it will be also in the days of the Son of Man: They ate, they drank, they married wives, they were given in marriage, until the day that Noah entered the ark, and the flood came and destroyed them all." Luke 17:26, 27.

You know how it was in the days of Noah. Business as usual. Then came that fatal surprise from the clear blue sky. All who had neglected God's warning paid for it with their lives. So will it be when Jesus breaks through the eastern sky. Corpses will be scattered across the earth like driftwood.

Do you realize that one day soon, within the space of a few short hours, this earth will be depopulated—empty—with not one human being left alive, anywhere in the world? When God decides it's closing time, He will lock up this planet and leave it empty, uninhabited—without even a For Rent sign! We find a vivid picture of this desolate earth in the Old Testament book of Jeremiah.

We have all heard the gloomy predictions about how this world would look after a nuclear war. A dismal gray wasteland. Jeremiah's description of our planet after Jesus comes bears striking resemblance to the eerie scene scientists warn us about: "I beheld the earth, and indeed it was without form, and void; and the heavens, they had no light. I beheld the mountains, and indeed they trembled, and all the hills moved back and forth. I beheld, and indeed there was no man, and all the birds of the heavens had fled. I beheld, and indeed the fruitful land was a wilderness, and all its cities were broken down at the presence of the Lord, by His fierce anger. For thus says the Lord: 'The whole land shall be desolate; yet I will not make a full end.' " Jeremiah 4:23-27.

The prophet describes the earth as without form and void. Just as in the first chapter of Genesis, before Creation was complete. We also read that the earth will be dark. The heavens have no light. No human life remains; even the birds have fled.

Evidently sinners won't have a second chance. When Christ returns, all will have had their last chance. And that is it.

Is this morbid scene the final chapter of earth's history? No, friend, it is not. Did you notice the ray of hope? God promises, "Yet I will not make a full end." Evidently He still has plans for this planet.

Now, where will Satan spend the thousand years of earth's emptiness? In Revelation 20:1-3 we learn the devil will be exiled, confined to this earth with no one to tempt. "I saw an angel coming down from heaven, having the key to the bottomless pit and a great chain in his hand. He laid hold of the dragon, that serpent of old, who is the Devil and Satan, and bound him for a thousand years; and he cast him into the bottomless pit, and shut him up, and set a seal on him, so that he should deceive the nations no more till the thousand years were finished. But after these things he must be released for a little while."

There is no way to lock up Satan with a literal key or restrain him with a real chain. And no bottomless pit, no yawning chasm, could hold him. So what could this mean? Simply a symbolic way of saying that Satan will at last be stopped. He and his angels will be confined on this earth. Today Satan roams as a roaring lion, looking for people to devour with temptation. See 1 Peter 5:8. But after Jesus comes, every human being will be either dead or gone. The great rebel will have nothing to do for a thousand years. Except to wander over the dark, desolate earth amid the havoc he has caused.

But did you notice that the devil will be loosed again after his thousand-year vacation? This means he'll have his wicked followers back. We read on: "Now when the thousand years have expired, Satan will be released from his prison and will go out to deceive the nations which are in the four corners of the earth, Gog and Magog, to gather them together to battle, whose number is as the sand of the sea." Revelation 20:7, 8.

After the thousand years, things happen rapidly. Satan, loosed by the resurrection of the lost, once again controls the rebel host. What happens next? The drama unfolds in verse 9: "They went up on the breadth of the earth and surrounded the camp of the saints and the beloved city. And fire came down from God out of heaven and devoured them."

How did the Holy City, the camp of the saints get down here? Remember that in the last chapter we learned that the heavenly city, with all God's people in it, will travel through space to this planet. Then everyone who has ever lived will be alive, inside or outside the city.

Picture the scene. Satan compares the vast host under his command with the much smaller number within the city. Numbers favor his side. And he has military leaders from all history behind him. Hitler is there too. Satan rallies his forces for a final frenzied attack on God's throne. The vast rebel army advances toward the city.

Then what happens? Hell happens. Hell—as the Bible describes it—happens. Fire streaks down from above. The earth becomes a vast, seething lake of fire. But the city of God rides safely upon it—just as Noah's ark was protected during the waters of the Flood.

Hell will be hot. So hot, sin and sinners will not survive. But after those flames have done their work, they will go out. Just as the water receded in Noah's day, the lake of fire subsides. Then God brings beauty out of ashes. He restores this earth as beautiful as long-lost Eden. See 2 Peter 3:13.

Rebellion will be over, never to trouble a happy universe again. Sin will be gone—and with it death and pain and heartache. Finally Jesus fulfills His promise that the meek will inherit the earth. See Matthew 5:5. God will give this born-again planet to His people as their permanent home.

No eternally burning hell will pollute our new earth paradise. True, the *results* of hellfire will be eternal. There is no recovery from it—no resurrection from final, second death. But the suffering of the lost won't spoil our everlasting joy. Aren't you glad the lost will not suffer eternally?

These days many are urging stiffer punishment for criminals—even the death penalty for murderers. But I've never heard anyone suggest prolonged torture for any criminal, no matter how terrible the crime. Tell me, are we more kind than God? Sometimes I've wondered whether we feel that criminals themselves can be kinder than God.

Back in the summer of 1976, the people of Chowchilla, California, were stunned by the kidnapping of twenty-six local children. It happened at 4:15 the afternoon of July 15. Bus driver Ed Ray was returning with the children from a summer-school outing. Suddenly, up ahead, he saw a white van blocking the road. Ed hit the brakes and stopped. Three masked men, brandishing pistols and sawed-off shotguns, ordered him to the back of the bus with the children.

As you can imagine, the poor children were terrified. Some sat stunned. Others cried, pleaded, or fainted. Ed Ray tried to calm them down. But how could he hide his own fear? What were these masked men going to do with them?

Hiding the bus behind a thicket of tall bamboo, the kidnappers transferred the hostages into two vans. After a terrifying eleven-hour trip, they finally bumped to a stop. The bewildered, frightened children stumbled out. Guns pointed to a three-foot hole in the ground. They obeyed and Ed Ray was given a flashlight and forced in behind them. The hole was sealed with a metal plate, weighted down with giant truck batteries, and finally covered with dirt. The horrified captives were entombed alive!

Ed's flashlight showed that they were inside a buried moving van. The kidnappers had made quite elaborate preparations for their victims. Mattresses, Cheerios, potato chips, a couple of loaves of bread, and plenty of water. There were two improvised toilets. And, most important, two plastic ventilation pipes. Even fans.

The captives spent sixteen hours buried in their grave. Finally Ed, with the help of the boys, dug through to daylight. Ed Ray was a hero! And how Chowchilla cheered!

Listen. There are millions of Christians who think God is not as thoughtful as those kidnappers were. Are even some criminals kinder than God? Perish the thought!

Back in Noah's day, when the people drowned, they were gone. God did not keep them endlessly thrashing about in the water. And the citizens of Sodom and Gomorrah are not still burning there beneath the Dead Sea. But did you know the Bible says that the citizens of Sodom and Gomorrah were destroyed by "eternal fire"? Those are the very words. Listen. "Sodom and Gomorrah . . . are set forth as an example, suffering the vengeance of eternal fire." Jude 7.

Eternal fire. Eternal in its effect, you see. The *punishment* is everlasting—but not the *punishing*. Remember, the wages of sin is death. Not eternal life in hell. Death means the absence of life, the absence of existence. So the doctrine of eternal hell isn't seen in Scripture, no matter how many sincere people may have thought it to be so. It's tradition. A holdover from the Dark Ages.

Here is an interesting point to consider. On the cross, Jesus paid the wages of the whole world's sin by His death. Didn't He? Certainly! Did He suffer eternal torment? Of course not. Then to say sinners must be eternally punished suggests that Jesus failed to pay the full price of their sin. And we know that is not true!

Those who reject their Saviour's death will finally perish. For the good of the universe, for the good of everyone concerned, every trace of sin will be erased. God's eternal kingdom of peace will reign at last.

But what does the Bible mean about the smoke of their torment ascending up forever? Allow Scripture to explain its own terms. Did you know the Bible uses the word *forever* more than fifty times for things already ended? For instance, in 1 Samuel 1:22, we read that Hannah promised Samuel to the Lord "forever." Yet verse 28 explains, "As long as he lives he shall be lent to the Lord."

There you have it. As long as the wicked live, as long as consciousness lasts, they will burn. For some it may be just a few moments. Others will suffer longer. Yet even Hitler will finally heave his last gasp. Satan himself will perish at the end of the thousand years. That is what the record says. "You. . . shall be no more forever." Ezekiel 28:19.

You may wonder, "Why does God wait a thousand years to dispense with sin?" Simply this. God will not destroy the wicked until all the universe fully understands why—until you and I understand. So Paul speaks of a time when "the saints will judge the world." Remember? 1 Corinthians 6:2. During our thousand years in heaven, we will have time to examine God's dealings with loved ones who were lost. We will see God has indeed done all He could do to save each person. Then we will be prepared to witness the solemn and awful judgment of the lost.

Friend, think of the disappointment in the heart of the Saviour if you should be missing. No one could take your place. Not all the millions of the saved. Not all the adoring angels. Your Heavenly Father needs you there. Don't disappoint Him!

How God's heart will be crushed on the day of hellfire! Long ago Jesus cried over a doomed city. "O Jerusalem, Jerusalem . . ! How often I wanted to gather your children together, as a hen gathers her chicks under her wings, but you were not willing!" Matthew 23:37.

"O New York, how often I have stood beside your spires of steel and called out over Times Square and Broadway, but you would not hear!

"O London, how often My voice has blended with that of Big Ben, tolling the lateness of the hour. But you ignored My warning.

"O precious planet in rebellion, how patiently I have knocked at your hearts' doors, urging you to let Me in. I tried to save you from the burning. Yet you weren't willing! Now it's too late!"

But friend, today there's still time. Whether you realize it or not, this moment you are deciding whether to be inside or outside the Holy City. You do not have to be locked outside with Satan when the fire falls. You can be safely inside with the Lord Jesus Christ!

I think of the Australian lumberman who built a little cabin at the edge of the woods. One evening as he returned from work, a horrible scene met his sight. A forest fire had swept through and destroyed his little home. Only a smoking heap remained.

He wandered out to where the old chicken coop had stood. It too was a mass of ashes and burned wire. At his feet lay a mound of charred feathers. He idly kicked it over. And what do you suppose happened? Four little fuzzy babies scrambled out. Four little chicks survived, sheltered by their mother's love.

Friend, do you want to be covered when fire sweeps through this planet? You can be. You can be sheltered in your Saviour now.

Mutiny in Paradise

Starving babies. Orphaned children. Weeping widows. War-torn nations.

"If God is love—why?"

From countless broken hearts around the world comes the anguished cry, the angry demand, "Why, God? If You really love us, why don't You help us? If You are all powerful, why won't You stop our suffering? How did we ever get into this mess?"

Disturbing questions! Vital questions that deserve sane answers. Answers we will find in Revelation, the last book of the Bible.

So we launch into our fourth chapter focusing on the prophecies of Revelation. We will explore the story behind the great battle between good and evil raging throughout the prophecies of this fascinating book.

Really, this world did not have to turn out the way it did. Back in the beginning, when God gave us the Garden of Eden, there were no weapons. No pollutants. No prisons or hospitals. No need for soldiers or policemen—or preachers either! This planet emerged from its Creator's hand pure and perfect. And it was built to stay that way.

Well, whatever happened? It is the story of a planet in rebellion. A rebellion on earth that began with war in heaven. Yes—war in heaven, of all places! Let's read it now in Revelation 12:7-9. "War broke out in heaven: Michael and his angels fought against the dragon; and the dragon and his angels fought, but they did not prevail, nor was a place found for them in heaven any longer. So the great dragon was cast out, that serpent of old, called the Devil and Satan, who deceives the whole world; he was cast to the earth, and his angels were cast out with him."

Can you picture this cosmic drama? A mutiny in heaven! A revolt by Satan and his angels against the government of God. But the rebellion failed. The devil and his hosts were thrown out of heaven to this earth. But how did Satan come into existence in the first place? And where did he get his wicked angels? Did God create evil?

No. God created a perfect angel named Lucifer, who became the devil by his own choice. We find the story in Ezekiel chapter 28: "You were the anointed cherub who covers; I established you; you were on the holy mountain of God; you walked back and forth in the midst of fiery stones. You were perfect in your ways from the day you were created, till iniquity was found in you." "Your heart was lifted up because of your beauty; you corrupted your wisdom for the sake of your splendor; I cast you to the ground." Verses 14, 15, 17.

Do you see what happened? Lucifer, the one God anointed as head of the angels, became proud of himself. He abused the influence of his high authority to stir up trouble. So great were his deceptions that one third of heaven's angels joined his revolt. See Revelation 12:4.

How could a perfect angel start a rebellion? Was something wrong in the way God created Lucifer? No, rather, it was because God gave him freedom—power to choose his own way. God could have created a robot, programmed to be a puppet and obey without second thought. Or any thought at all. But God wouldn't do that. He loves His family and craves our willing love in return. And love cannot be commanded or programmed. We respond by free choice in appreciation of God's love.

Just as there can be no love without freedom, there can be no freedom without risk. Freedom brings opportunity for abuse. The same freedom that offers love can withhold it. The same exercise of choice that obeys can rebel. A dangerous risk indeed, this power to choose. But God was willing to risk His very throne for the sake of our freedom and love.

As Lucifer's insurrection ripened into active revolt, he attacked the throne of God. We read about it in Isaiah 14, beginning with verse 12: "How you are fallen from heaven, O Lucifer, son of the morning! How you are cut down to the ground. You who weakened the nations! For you have said in your heart: 'I will ascend into heaven, I will exalt my throne above the stars of God; I will also sit on the mount of the congregation on the farthest sides of the north; I will ascend above the heights of the clouds, I will be like the Most High.' " Verses 12-14.

For the good of the universe, God could not allow such a selfish tyrant to prevail in his power play. So He cast the devil out of heaven into exile on this planet. But why didn't God destroy the rebellion then and there? He could have saved Himself a lot of trouble. He could have saved Himself the cross!

But no, God let His rival live on for the benefit of the universe. Satan had claimed to offer a better government. The only way to expose this lie was to give the rebel the opportunity to prove his point and develop his principles. Only then could the universe fully see that God's way is best, that suffering and death await those who stray from His love.

Why was Satan exiled here, of all places? Because this world was soon to become the theater of the universe. God had a special plan for this planet. He wanted to populate our globe with human beings created in His image. God had many angels for company, but now He needed to start a family.

It shouldn't be hard for us to understand why God wanted children. What makes a couple with a double income interrupt their peace and prosperity for a precious, lovable, but sometimes restless little troublemaker? We may have friends, as God had angels, yet there's a hunger to have and hold children created in our image. A craving to love and care for our very own offspring. That's why God made us in His image, to somehow bear His likeness.

The Bible tells us that God breathed into Adam's nostrils the breath of life. Can't you picture our heavenly Father bending over His beloved offspring, tenderly sharing His own life?

By creating humanity in His image, God gave us freedom of choice. Not to ride the rail of His will like a locomotive, without a way of our own. Rather, as free moral agents, He gave us a steering wheel—the ability to do as we please. God knew we couldn't be happy unless we were free. And only through this freedom could we respond to His love.

In making us in His image, God took a further risk. He also gave us dominion—the responsibility to care for children of our own. You see the danger in this. Because if we ever went astray, everyone around us would suffer. A terrible risk indeed, this responsibility for others. But God knew we wouldn't feel fulfilled without it.

Then our Father lavished the finest that heaven could bestow upon His human family. He spared nothing. Picture the lush green meadows sprinkled with a rainbow of flowers. Rich fragrant forests. Clear running streams. The tree of life. And the other tree—the tree that offered death.

Why did God plant that tree of temptation there? To trap Adam and Eve? No. God presented this tree as a test of their trust and loyalty. He assured them that everything that could make them happy was already theirs through Him. But if they ever wished to doubt His leadership, someone else offered another option. Satan the serpent was eager to lure them away from their Father's love. The choice was theirs.

And the stakes were high. It was a life-or-death matter. If they ever left God, they would die, He warned. This was no arbitrary sentence. It was a basic fact of life. God is not only the Author but the Sustainer of life. Cut off from their source, humanity would have no more existence than a tree branch severed from its trunk. And if they sinned, the whole human race would be doomed. All their children and their children's children would be plunged into the grave.

And one sad day, it happened. You know the story. Our first parents succumbed to the fatal delusion that something was lacking in God's care, that God had withheld what the serpent would supply. Suddenly the relationship was shattered! God's precious children became strangers and orphans. By their own choice!

Sin took an immediate toll. Alienation and discord displaced harmony and happiness. Adam and Eve hid from God—or tried to. Reluctantly, God reminded them that they would have to die.

But then He surprised them with some good news which we call the gospel. Death would have to be, yes. But He would take their death upon Himself. He would pay the price with His own blood.

They must leave their garden home, but God would join them in their exile. Sweat and pain would be their lot, but God would hold their hands. And in the course of time He would come to this planet on His high-risk rescue mission.

How did He do it?

Jesus left the throne of heaven to be planted in the womb of a peasant girl. Imagine! The mighty Creator God became a creature, locked into time and space. Actually, it was God who worked in the carpenter's shop and joined our rat race. It was God who lived in poverty, who felt thirst from the noonday heat. It was God who got tired and slept in the storm-tossed boat. And it was all because He loved us and needed our friendship.

What kind of reception did God receive from us? The New Testament records the sad story that His own people refused to receive Him. Bitter disappointment! Yes, large crowds followed the Lord, but they mostly wanted to see His miracles and be healed of pain. Very few cared about His friendship.

A few disciples faithfully followed Him, but even they were too involved in their own power struggles to appreciate that God Himself was walking, talking, and sleeping with them. The night before His death, they argued about which of them ranked number one. They didn't even listen as Jesus tried to discuss His sacrifice for them the next morning. He had to wash their feet like a servant to win their attention and show them what it meant to be great.

The crisis occurred later that night in a garden called Gethsemane. Let's watch Jesus as He collapses under a deadly oppression which threatens to snuff out His life.

What is this strange smog choking His soul? It's the guilt of our sin. Our sins are clogging the lifeline with His Father that has sustained the Saviour on earth. As He ponders the price to be paid, He falls on His face in prayer: "My Father, if it's possible, take this cup of suffering away from Me! Yet not what I want—may Your will be done. But Father, if there's any other way We can save them, tell Me!" See Luke 22:42.

There isn't. So a crucial decision must now be made in the moonlit garden. Will He go through with it all? Or should guilty humanity bear its own deserved punishment?

Desperately needing the support of His disciples, He begs them to pray for Him. But they don't seem concerned. Worn out from their arguing, they fall fast asleep. Three times our Lord staggers back to hear some word of support or encouragement that the sacrifice of His soul would not be wasted. But each time He is greeted by their insensitive sleeping.

What pressure to give up and go back to heaven! And why not? His enemies are on the march to arrest Him. His friends don't seem to care. What good would it do to sacrifice Himself?

As Christ ponders what to do, the fate of humanity trembles in the balance. Finally, amid the bitterest agony, He makes the decision. Jesus will go to the cross! He will suffer the wrath of divine justice and satanic torment. He will pass through the grave to restore the shattered relationship with His sinful children.

As the mob makes its midnight arrest, the sleeping disciples awake. They get up and run away. All of them flee for their lives. Now the Son of God allows Himself to be handcuffed and rushed to court. There His enemies—those He came to save—condemn Him in the greatest travesty of justice this world has ever seen.

After being scourged till the blood spurts out, Christ is led away to a most painful and shameful death. His clothes are torn from Him. Now He hangs in open shame on the cruel cross. Maddened tormentors jeer the bleeding Lord as He writhes in agony. But far worse than the physical torment is the separation from His Father for our sin. In sheer terror He cries, "My God, My God, why have You forsaken Me?"

Why, God? Jesus wonders too!

Tell me, friend, Why *did* the Father in heaven have to forsake His Son? So He could accept you and me! Listen to this sublime passage from Ellen White's inspired book *The Desire of Ages,* pp. 755, 756.

"The spotless Son of God hung upon the cross, His flesh lacerated with stripes; those hands so often reached out in blessing, nailed to the wooden bars; those feet so tireless on ministries of love, spiked to the tree; that royal head pierced by the crown of thorns; those quivering lips shaped to the cry of woe. And all that He endured—the blood drops that flowed from His head, His hands, His feet, the agony that racked His frame, and the unutterable anguish that filled His soul at the hiding of His Father's face—speaks to each child of humanity, declaring, it is for thee that the Son of God consents to bear this burden of guilt; for thee He spoils the domain of death, and opens the gates of Paradise. He who stilled the angry waves and walked the foam-capped billows, who made devils tremble and disease flee, who opened blind eyes and called forth the dead to life— offers Himself upon the cross as a sacrifice, and this from love to thee. He, the Sin Bearer, endures the wrath of divine justice, and for thy sake becomes sin itself."

Christ had done no wrong. But as our stand-in and substitute, He took our punishment. He was pronounced guilty, so we could be declared forgiven and live with Him forever.

Christ is crucified between two thieves. They join the crowd in hurling insults at the Saviour. But one of them begins to realize that something out of place is happening. Someone innocent is dying—a Saviour dying for his own sin. Hope springs within his breast. Maybe it's not too late! Desperately he casts himself upon the mercy of the One he so recently mocked. Quickly, acceptance comes. The dying Saviour promises a place in paradise to a dying thief.

As Jesus dies, He declares in triumph, "It is finished!" Mission accomplished! Humanity redeemed! Children of God again!

No more fearful hiding, like Adam and Eve in the shame of their sin. We've been adopted! Our heavenly Father wants us home. Will you come? Will you accept His gift of salvation as more precious than anything else you know? The choice is yours.

By His life and death, Christ won back all that was lost. Soon He will restore everything the human race once enjoyed in Eden. Let's take a few moments as we close our study to preview the paradise home Jesus promised. You'll find the description in Revelation 21, verses 1 to 5:

"And I saw a new heaven and a new earth, for the first heaven and the first earth had passed away. Also there was no more sea. Then I, John, saw the holy city, New Jerusalem, coming down out of heaven from God, prepared as a bride adorned for her husband. And I heard a loud voice from heaven saying, 'Behold, the tabernacle of God is with men, and He will dwell with them, and they shall be His people, and God Himself will be with them and be their God. And God will wipe every tear from their eyes; there shall be no more death, nor sorrow, nor crying; and there shall be no more pain, for the former things have passed away.' Then He that sat on the throne said, 'Behold, I make all things new.' "

Think of it, friend—all things new! And it's all for you! What are you going to do about it?

As we consider our response to God's love, I'm reminded of the little poodle who felt trapped inside his master's house. Envying the kids outside building a snowman, he longs for an opportunity to run free. Finally he manages to slip out the door.

Delighted to be loose at last, he dashes back and forth across the yard and around and around the snowman. But soon his little legs get cold. His enthusiasm shivers away. Finally he concludes that, be it ever so humdrum, there's no place like home. Its confinement offers warmth and security. Colder and wiser, he whimpers on the doorstep. Of course, his master lets the repentant little fellow back inside.

Tell me, friend, are you like that poodle? Tired of running in circles outside the Father's warm house? Shivering with guilt and shame? Then come inside your heavenly Father's house where it's warm. Live in His love and be safe evermore.

When the Red Phone Rings

October 1962. A crisis over Cuba. Enemy missiles lurking in America's front yard!

President Kennedy responds with a daring naval blockade. Yet Soviet ships steam relentlessly forward. It's a terrifying superpower showdown! Suddenly we find ourselves poised on the brink of World War III. The world holds its breath. Finally the Russians back down.

It was a narrow escape. But what will happen next time?

After the close call over Cuba, both superpowers saw the need for directly communicating in a crisis. Instantly. Accurately. So in August of 1963 they linked Washington and Moscow with a hotline.

The red phone, as we call it now, has served us well. Its first use came in 1967 during the frantic moments of the Six-Day War. During the next clash between the Arabs and Israelis, the hotline buzzed again. Few Americans understood the danger of that October 1973 crisis. How close the superpowers edged toward war.

We still depend upon the hotline. It is our last resort against doomsday. Do you recall Walter Mondale's campaign commercial with the ringing red phone? His point was that America needs experienced leadership to avoid nuclear war.

Of course, we need leaders we can trust. But who really runs the red phone? We've been to the brink of World War III time and again. Yet business continues as usual. Is some supernatural power holding back the winds of strife? If so, for how long? In Revelation 7, beginning with verse 1, we find out.

"After these things I saw four angels standing at the four corners of the earth, holding the four winds of the earth, that the wind should not blow on the earth, on the sea, or on any tree. Then I saw another angel ascending from the east, having the seal of the living God. And he cried with a loud voice to the four angels to whom it was granted to harm the earth and the sea, saying, 'Do not harm the earth, the sea, or the trees till we have sealed the servants of our God on their foreheads.' " Revelation 7:1-3.

Winds on a leash! Angels holding back the winds of war and destruction. Containing the nuclear threat. Forbidding history to sign out just yet.

Why does God delay the end of the world? Because something must first happen with His people. We must receive the seal of the living God before Jesus comes. Evidently this business of being sealed is pretty important. Shall we probe it further?

Revelation 7 goes on to describe how 144,000 saints will be sealed. Twelve thousand from each of the twelve tribes of Israel.

This number twelve shows completeness. A complete year has twelve months. Christ called twelve apostles. The Holy City has twelve pearly gates. And Old Testament Israel began with twelve distinct tribes.

But then the various tribes intermarried among themselves. Today it would probably be impossible to find exactly 12,000 pure-blooded members of each of the old twelve tribes. So this reference to Israel must be symbolic. Who are the real children of Israel now?

According to the New Testament, believers in Jesus are God's chosen people. Not through their national origin. But because of their faith in Christ. All God's promises to Abraham belong to Christians today. In Jesus we become the new Israel. See Galatians 3:29.

So the symbolic 144,000 Israelites, or God's followers actually, represent the complete family of all believers at the end of the world. The great multitude from all nations who overcome earth's final crisis. Those who receive God's seal.

A friend of mine shared a personal experience that helps me understand what it means to be sealed. As a boy he attended a little country school. Thirteen students in eight grades in one room. The teacher was a seventeen-year-old girl, fresh out of school. As you can imagine, she had her hands full keeping law and order. Soon her struggle to maintain discipline became a losing battle.

One afternoon outside the schoolhouse my friend joined his peers in complaining about classes. He voiced his dislike for the teacher. How much he hated her rules. How much he wished she would go away.

Just then he happened to glance through the open window. There stood that poor teacher, her shoulders quivering with sobs. The sight of her sorrow pierced him like a sword. He realized now that misbehavior meant more than breaking a rule. He had broken a heart. Overwhelmed with remorse and repentance, he determined to become a new boy. And he did!

Friend, this is the experience of God's people who are sealed. They have learned that indulging in sin means more than breaking God's law. It also breaks His heart. And they resolve to die rather than do that. We see this attitude of God's people in Hebrews 8. Let's read verse 10.

" 'This is the covenant that I will make with the house of Israel: After those days,' says the Lord, 'I will put My laws in their mind and write them on their hearts; and I will be their God, and they shall be My people.' " Hebrews 8:10.

A willing mind in harmony with God's law. This is what it means to have heaven's seal upon your forehead.

Come with me back to Revelation. In chapter 14 we meet the symbolic 144,000 again. This time they have God's name on their foreheads. In Bible days parents chose names to represent the character they wanted their children to have. Today we usually pick names to honor relatives or other favorite people. Or we like the sound of the name. But whether we know it or not, even now each name has its own special meaning.

Can you guess what my name, George, means? "Tiller of the ground. Farmer." My wife Nellie's name means "possessor of feminine virtues." What does your name mean? Go down to the library sometime and look it up. See whether your name actually represents your character.

The sealed saints who bear God's name reflect His character. His faithful love. They are not defiled by hypocrisy. Instead they remain pure as virgins in their relationship with God. And they obey His commandments. Notice verse 12: "Here is the patience of the saints; here are those who keep the commandments of God and the faith of Jesus."

Faith in Jesus. Keeping God's commandments. They go together in receiving the seal. God waits while we learn how to trust and obey. We discover more about these sealed saints in the message they believe. Revelation 14, verses 6 and 7:

"I saw another angel flying in the midst of heaven, having the everlasting gospel to preach to those who dwell on the earth—to every nation, tribe, tongue, and people—saying with a loud voice, 'Fear God and give glory to Him, for the hour of His judgment has come; and worship Him who made heaven and earth, the sea and springs of water.' "

An angel with a message. Calling the whole world to worship the Creator. To prepare for judgment. To accept salvation.

Some say the gospel belongs to the New Testament. But notice that it is called the "everlasting gospel." It has been with us from the day sin invaded our planet.

Picture the scene in the Garden of Eden. Adam and Eve linger under the tree, savoring the flavor of forbidden fruit. Suddenly chills race up their spines. Icy pangs of guilt and shame. Shivering in their nakedness, they hunt for refuge in the depths of the forest. As they crouch amid their lush green prison, terror overwhelms them. They remember God's warning. On the day they sinned, they must die. And here He comes to kill them!

But no. God doesn't strike them dead. Instead, He tenderly covers their shame with the skin of an animal. What is happening here? Why does He let them live?

Or did they really die that day after all? Think this through. What must you do to get a garment of skin? You must kill. An innocent animal, probably a lamb, perished in place of the condemned couple. Because a substitute died their death, they could live. A happy life, free from shame and guilt.

You know who that substitute symbolized. Our Lord Jesus Christ, the great Lamb of God. He offers us salvation as a gift. Free, but not cheap. It cost His death on the cross.

This is the everlasting gospel. The foundation of Christianity. And we found it way back at the gates of the Garden of Eden.

Like a refreshing mountain stream, the gospel runs clear through the Old Testament. Take the experience of Abraham and his son Isaac. As they trudge up Mount Moriah, the mountain of sacrifice, the aged father trembles at the thought of losing his only son. Then he remembers the gospel: "My son, God will provide for Himself the lamb for a burnt offering." Genesis 22:8. God Himself provides the sacrifice for sin. That was their hope way back in Genesis! And that is our hope today.

Unfortunately, Abraham's descendants forgot the gospel. So God brought them to Mount Sinai and taught them the meaning of sacrifice. Every bleeding lamb on the altar reminded them to trust in the blood of their Saviour to come.

At Mount Sinai God reminded them of something else. We find it in Exodus 20. Way back at creation, God had given His children a weekly reminder to trust in Him. Let's read about it, beginning with verse 8: "Remember the Sabbath day, to keep it holy. Six days you shall labor and do all your work, but the seventh day is the Sabbath of the Lord your God. In it you shall do no work. . . . For in six days the Lord made the heavens and the earth, the sea, and all that is in them, and rested the seventh day. Therefore the Lord blessed the Sabbath day and hallowed it." Verses 8-11.

"Remember the Sabbath." Why? Because the Sabbath calls us to cease from our works and rest in God's work for us. He finished creation in six days and rested the seventh. Then He invited His children—who deserved nothing—to share the celebration of His work.

The Sabbath commandment differs from the other nine. All the other commandments tell us what we must do for God and neighbor. But the Sabbath points us away from human works. To rest in God's work for us. And that's the gospel! Without Sabbath rest, our obedience would be legalism.

Come reverently with me now to Calvary. It's late Friday afternoon, almost time to welcome the Sabbath. Jesus, hanging on the cross, recalls all He has done for our salvation. Then, with His dying breath, He proclaims, "It is finished!" Mission accomplished! Mankind redeemed!

Again Jesus rests from His work on the Sabbath, just as He did after creation. Only this time in the tomb. Following Sabbath rest, Christ arises and ascends to heaven's throne.

Can you see how the Sabbath is the greatest teaching tool of the gospel? The brightest of billboards proclaiming Calvary's freedom? Week by week it reminds us that we can't save ourselves—we must trust Jesus. And in this world cursed by atheism, the Sabbath testifies that we didn't evolve by chance. God created us. We're His children.

We turn now to Exodus 31. Can you see why Jesus proclaimed Himself "Lord of the Sabbath"? Because it commemorates His two greatest acts on our behalf—creating us and saving us. We show our faith in Jesus, our Maker and Redeemer, by resting on the seventh day. The Sabbath seals our relationship with Him. We see this here in verse 13: "Surely My Sabbaths you shall keep, for it is a sign between Me and you throughout your generations, that you may know that I am the Lord who sanctifies you."

So the Sabbath is the sign between God and His people. At creation God "sanctified" the seventh day. That is, He set it apart from other days of the week. And now, through the Sabbath, God sets us apart from the world to seal us as His own.

But most of us don't want to be set apart from the world. We would rather fit in with the crowd. Why this strange urge to conform?

Why are we terrified about being different? Where is the fervent individualism that made the heroes and the martyrs of the past? What happened to the excitement of taking one's stand? We seem to be hypnotized with the childhood game of follow-the-leader.

Margaret Applegarth has written a delightful book called *Men as Trees Walking*. In it she tells the story, true but almost unbelievable, of Jean Henri Fabre and his study of the processionary caterpillar.

It seems that this caterpillar wanders about aimlessly, pursued by many followers who move when he moves, stop when he stops, and eat when he eats. Pine needles are their principal source of food.

One day Fabre tried an experiment. He filled a flowerpot with pine needles, which they love, and then lined up the caterpillars in a solid ring around the rim of the pot. Sure enough, they began to move slowly around and around the rim, each following the one ahead. And yes, you've guessed it. They continued this senseless revolving for seven days, never once stopping for food—until one by one they began to collapse.

No. It is not always safe to follow the crowd. To have followed the public mood in Christ's day would have been to reject Him. Listen to the report of the officers sent out to arrest Jesus, but returning without Him. "The officers answered, 'No man ever spoke like this Man!' Then the Pharisees answered them, 'Are you also deceived? Have any of the rulers or the Pharisees believed in Him?' " John 7:46-48.

This was the question that discouraged so many from following Jesus. They had been deeply moved by Christ's message. But when reminded that the religious leaders had rejected Him, they surrendered conscience and forfeited faith. Do we have that problem today?

Truth still burns its conviction into human hearts. It may be startling truth. It may seem strange to modern ears. It may concern the day God says to remember. And there are those who ask, "Have the respected leaders of our day accepted it? Has it been received into the mainstream of religious thought?"

Sabbath rest, you see, sets God's people apart from the world. You might say it keeps us from becoming processionary caterpillars! Not that the seventh day has any value in itself. It's rather what the day represents. Let me illustrate what I mean.

Take a piece of red cloth. It's not worth much by itself. But add some white cloth and some blue cloth and sew them all together into the Tricolor of France. Frenchmen will die for their flag! Sew them together into the Union Jack, and Britishers will lay down their lives for it. And if you sew those ordinary pieces of cloth into the Stars and Stripes, Americans will die for it!

Just so, God took an ordinary day. But then He set it apart from other days of the week and made the Sabbath. He made it represent the greatest things He's done for us. The reasons why we worship Him.

Remember that angel's message in Revelation 14? It repeats the very words of the Sabbath commandment: "Worship Him who made heaven and earth."

So the Sabbath stands at the foundation of true worship. A test of our willingness to serve God.

You can imagine how Satan hates the Sabbath. Because it is the sign of our relationship with God. And the devil does not want us to be sealed. He does not want us to be free.

Back in the old days, on the shores of the Mississippi, Abraham Lincoln stood near the market for slave trading. He watched the tragic sight of families torn apart. Their heartbreaking sobs pierced his soul. Clenching his fists, he vowed, "If I ever get a chance to hit this, I'll hit it hard." And he did.

Before Lincoln's great emancipation, a slave named Joe was shoved on the auction block. Bitter and resentful, he muttered, "I won't work! I won't work!" But a wealthy landowner purchased him anyway.

He led Joe to the carriage, and they drove out of town to the plantation. There by a lake stood a little bungalow. With curtains, flowers, and a cobblestone walkway. The new master stopped the carriage. Turning to Joe, he smiled. "Here's your new home. You don't have to work for it. I've bought you to set you free."

For a moment Joe sat stunned. Then his eyes filled with tears. Overwhelmed, he exclaimed, "Master, I'll serve you forever."

One day long ago Someone from a land far away looked down on this earth. He saw our bondage to Satan and heard our cry for freedom. He determined, "Someday I'll get a chance to hit that, and I'll hit it hard." Jesus did just that. By His death He set us free.

And He has prepared a wonderful place for us. Beautiful beyond our wildest imagination. Soon He will return to take us home. To be with Him forever.

Oh, friend. Will you serve Him forever?

The Antichrist Exposed

The antichrist. We've been warned, and we've been waiting. Who in the world will it be? A religious fanatic like the Ayatollah Khomeini? Or a political tyrant like Idi Amin? A cult leader such as Sun Myung Moon? Perhaps an atheist like Madalyn Murray O'Hair?

The antichrist. Is it a human or a demon? A government? Maybe even a church?

Fascinated and frightened. That's how we feel about the mysteries of the antichrist. We're also quite confused. Bookstores, even drugstores, feature a smorgasbord of paperback religious thrillers. Each comes spiced with new speculation about the beast.

How can we know what's truth? We'd better get the facts straight from the source, wouldn't you say? Why don't we open our Bibles to Revelation 13—the so-called "beast chapter." Let's read chapter 13, verses 1 and 2:

"I stood on the sand of the sea. And I saw a beast rising up out of the sea, having seven heads and ten horns, and on his horns ten crowns, and on his heads a blasphemous name. Now the beast which I saw was like a leopard, his feet were like the feet of a bear, and his mouth like the mouth of a lion. And the dragon gave him his power, his throne, and great authority."

A strange beast indeed, this antichrist power. With a body from a leopard, a bear, and a lion. Perhaps you've studied those animals before in the Old Testament book of Daniel. We learn from Scripture decoding that they represent three kingdoms—

4—R.F.A.

three ancient kingdoms, in fact—Babylon, Persia, and Greece. Followed, of course, by the Roman Empire.

So this blasphemous beast of Revelation 13 sums up the great world empires of Old Testament history. What religion did those heathen empires have in common? Sun worship.

Adoration of the sun can be traced all the way back to the time of Noah. Nimrod, his great-grandson, became a "mighty one on the earth." Genesis 10:8. Beginning with his Tower of Babel, Nimrod's achievements adorn the records and legends of ancient history. But this talented leader was evil. A father of false worship.

False worship also thrived through Ishtar, called the queen of heaven, goddess of love and fertility. Ishtar, according to legend, gave birth to a son Tammuz, without a father. Here in pagan sun worship, centuries before Christ, we find a counterfeit of the virgin birth. Imagine! Certain of the male gods of fertility became sun gods. They all died every winter and had to be resurrected to restore the fertility of plants, animals, and humans.

Sun worship from ancient Babylon spread to infect the world. Ancient records and art forms show how each nation reverenced the sun in the customs of its own culture. But why did they worship the sun? Well, the sun brings light, warmth, growth—what we need for life itself. Reigning supreme over nature, the sun would be the natural object of worship for those who reject their Creator.

Ceremonies to honor the sun god were gruesome beyond belief. Babies were burned as living sacrifices. Young women were degraded as sun temple prostitutes. All to appease the endless appetite of sun dieties rather than to accept the Creator's gift of salvation.

Time and again God exposed the follies of sun worship. Remember the story of how He rescued His people from Egypt? How He overpowered the sun with three days of darkness? All who turned from the sun god and put the lamb's blood on their doorpost were saved from the death angel. Even so, Israel exported sun idolatry in the Exodus. The golden calf they reverenced represented Apis, an image closely associated with sun worship.

Throughout Old Testament times adoration of the sun sup-
planted true worship in Israel. King Solomon, the very one who
built God's temple, defiled Jerusalem with paganism. Sun worship flourished. The eighth chapter of Ezekiel records the
shocking scene of women reverencing Tammuz in the temple.
And men bowing low before the sun.

Can you imagine! Pagan worship in God's own temple! But
faithful prophets called Israel away from the sun to their Creator. They pointed to the seventh-day Sabbath, God's weekly
reminder of Creation. Yet the Hebrews persisted in paganism.
Finally the Lord gave them up to be captives in Babylon, that
ancient center of sun worship. At last God's people learned
their lesson.

But they then went to the other extreme. After returning
from Babylon, they shunned their pagan neighbors to avoid
contamination. By the time of Christ, the Jews had largely
quarantined themselves from the Gentiles around them.

Meanwhile, after Babylon fell to the Persians, sun worship
continued to spread. And when Alexander the Great conquered
the then-known world, the Greeks introduced their own sophis-
ticated brand of idolatry. Including reverence for the sun.

And, of course, the Romans venerated the sun in their empire. They named the days of the week according to their heathen religion. Sunday they reverenced the sun. Monday the
Moon. Tuesday, Mars. Wednesday, Mercury. Thursday they
honored Jupiter. Friday, Venus. Saturday? You guessed it—
Saturn. Just as the sun rules over the planets, Sunday rose to
honor above other days in the week.

But true Christians of the first century nobly refused any
part of pagan worship. And as a result they suffered horrible
persecution. Thousands were thrown to the lions or burned
alive. Yet the church stood firm. Satan, failing to overcome
God's people through force, then tried a new strategy. He determined to infiltrate Christianity through paganism. Little by
little he mingled the ceremonies of sun worship with Bible
truth.

Now why would the church be attracted to paganism? For
one thing, Christians wanted to distance themselves from any-

thing seeming to be Jewish. Jews, you see, had put themselves in the emperor's doghouse. They hated Roman authority. Constantly they revolted to regain their own national rule.

And Rome struck back. In A.D. 49 Emperor Claudius expelled the Jews from Rome for their constant rioting. See Acts 18:2. Things got worse. Strict sanctions were enjoined upon Jews. They responded by refusing to pray for God's blessing on the emperor. Rome considered this treason.

So in A.D. 70 Roman armies stormed Jerusalem. A quarter of a million Jews were starved, burned, crucified, or otherwise killed. Their glorious temple lay in ruins. Numerous anti-Jewish riots swept the empire, climaxed by even stiffer penalties for Jews.

You see, because Christians shared the same heritage as Jews, Romans tended to treat both groups the same. This was unfair, of course. Christians wanted peace with the emperor, rendering to Caesar his due. Yet they suffered just as if they were Jews. No wonder Christians cut themselves off from everything remotely Jewish. You can see why they craved a new identity more favorable with the empire.

And now with Jerusalem destroyed, Christians looked to the capital city as their new church center. By A.D. 95 Clement, bishop of Rome, had become quite prominent. His epistles commanded respect among believers. Some in the churches even considered them inspired. Rome's influence in the church increased further after the second destruction of Jerusalem in A.D. 135. Emperor Hadrian outlawed Jewish worship, particularly their Sabbath keeping. So Christians felt compelled to divorce themselves completely from their Hebrew heritage. Although believers withstood outright idolatry—even to the point of death—pagan symbols and ceremonies slipped in the back door. Heathen holidays became Christian holy days.

Tell me. Have you ever wondered what Easter eggs and bunny rabbits have to do with the resurrection of Christ? Nothing, of course. They were pagan symbols of fertility. But the church adopted them to celebrate new life in Jesus. The *Encyclopedia Britannica* states, "Christianity . . . incorporated in its celebration of the great Christian feast day [Easter] many of the heathen rites and customs of the Spring festival."

Other heathen feasts besides Easter infiltrated the church. For centuries pagans celebrated the birth of their sun god Tammuz on December 25. Have you ever heard of that date?

Now there's nothing morally wrong with exchanging gifts at Christmas time—even if that isn't the true date of Christ's birth. Or hiding Easter eggs or putting bunnies in baskets for children. But here is my question. Since our Christian holidays originally came to us tainted with sun worship, how do we know that other areas of our worship, even truths morally vital, have not been tampered with too? Think about it.

So it was that Christians, seeking some relief from persecution, welcomed the rituals of sun worship. Of course, nobody suggests they actually worshiped the sun. They were simply celebrating Christ's birth and resurrection. So they reasoned.

Now this development did not happen in a corner. Scholars recognize these pagan roots in Christianity. No less an authority than Cardinal John Henry Newman tells the facts in his book *The Development of the Christian Religion:* "Temples, incense, oil lamps, votive offerings, holy water, holidays and seasons of devotion, processions, blessing of fields, sacerdotal vestments, the tonsure, and images . . . are all of pagan origin."—Page 359.

Now what do you think of that?

And, on the other hand, pagans actually became comfortable with Christianity. And why not? They could celebrate their heathen holidays in the name of Jesus. But a price had been paid. Pure faith lay buried deep in pagan tradition. Accommodation took the place of transformation. Diversion all too often replaced conversion.

By the fourth century, Christianity so resembled paganism that the emperor found it easy to become a believer. Constantine the Great proclaimed himself a convert in the year 312. Persecution ceased. Outright pagan sacrifices were outlawed. Christian worship became official. Delighted church leaders pledged to support the new Christian regime. Hand in hand, church and state mixed faith in Christ with sun-worship rituals. On March 7, 321, Constantine ordered his empire to reverence the "venerable day of the sun." Not the Son of God, you understand, but the sun. The day of pagan sun worship.

Sunday keeping by Christians was nothing new. Sometimes after Hadrian's second-century persecution of the Jews, the church in Rome had exchanged the Bible Sabbath for Sunday. So with Constantine's seal of approval, the day of the sun increased in importance to the church. In 538 a council at Orleans, France, forbade all work on the first day of the week. Eventually laws became so strict that a woman could be sentenced to seven days' penance for washing her hair on Sunday.

Sunday largely eclipsed the Sabbath in the western part of the empire, but in the east quite a few still worshiped on the seventh day. Many kept both days holy. Pockets of Sabbath keepers remained in areas known now as Egypt, Tunisia, Turkey, Palestine, and Syria. Also Ethiopia, Armenia, and Yugoslavia. Even in Ireland. Later—as late as the fifth century—evidence suggests that, Saint Patrick kept the seventh day holy.

Those who honored the Bible Sabbath found themselves in mortal danger. Anyone who accepted the Bible as the only rule of faith and who insisted upon Jesus alone as intercessor qualified as a heretic. The burning of heretics began at Orleans, France, in 1022. Persecution intensified during the great Crusades. Then came the infamous Inquisition, when the state enforced the teachings of the church. Thousands lost their lives for their simple faith in Christ.

These were dark ages for the church. How could Christians be so intolerant of their brothers and sisters in Christ? Jesus had predicted that those who killed His followers would sincerely think they were serving God. See John 16:2. Officials believed killing heretics saved thousands of others from following them into eternal torment. Even the heretics themselves might repent through fear of the flames. At least that's what many religious leaders hoped for.

It is not for us to question the motives of our medieval ancestors. Would it not be better to pray with our Saviour, "Father, forgive them, for they know not what they do"? Nor must we overlook the good done by the church. Throughout the world monasteries provided care for orphans, widows, and the sick. And all of us owe appreciation to the church of the Middle Ages for preserving the Scriptures.

Unfortunately, however, the Bibles were chained to monastery walls. Common people had to learn secondhand from the clergy. Knowledge of the Bible became scarce. Without question, the church was ripe for reform.

Should this erosion of Christian faith surprise us? After all, hadn't God's people in Old Testament times continually succumbed to false worship? The New Testament predicted that history would repeat itself. Apostasy would prevail in the church. The apostle Peter warned, "There will be false teachers among you, who will secretly bring in destructive heresies. . . . And many will follow their destructive ways." 2 Peter 2:1, 2.

Long ago, God's enemy learned a lesson. He had tried first to crush Christianity with persecution. It didn't work. So he resorted to deception. Quietly, gradually, he infiltrated the church with the trappings of sun worship. That *did* work.

Which do you think would be most deceptive today? Straightforward persecution? Or subtle infiltration—counterfeiting Christianity from within?

Today certain atheistic countries are waging open warfare against Christianity. Millions of persecuted believers stand brave and strong, while others forfeit their faith. But very few are deceived. It's easy to know what the enemy is up to when he threatens to throw you in jail for your faith.

Is the enemy using atheism now as a smoke screen? Is he diverting our attention as he undermines us with subtle change? Could it be that all the time we've been scouting the horizon for the antichrist, he has been growing in our own backyard?

Perhaps we ought to take another look at the meaning of the word *antichrist*. That could be our problem. *Anti,* means "against" or "instead of"—either to oppose Christ openly or to subtly overshadow Him. Which of these two types of warfare against Christ do we see in the antichrist?

In Thessalonians 2, verse 3 we read : "Let no one deceive you by any means; for that Day will not come unless the falling away comes first, and the man of sin is revealed, the son of perdition."

"Let no one deceive you," says the apostle. So deception is involved. No question about it. Evidently the antichrist results in a "falling away," a gradual apostasy within the body of believers. Didn't Jesus Himself warn about deception—about a wolf in sheep's clothing?

The antichrist. Dedicated men at different times reached the same conclusion. Martin Luther. John Knox, the Scottish Reformer. King James I, who commissioned our King James Bible. Sir Isaac Newton, the famous scientist and Bible student. Even the Puritan preacher John Cotton, known as the Patriarch of New England. Were they all mistaken? Or did they know something we've overlooked? And their conclusions you will not find in the many paperbacks professing to explain the antichrist which are found in the bookstores today.

So let's turn back to Revelation 13 and test the conclusions of the Reformers. You recall that the beast there has ten horns. Did the Roman empire collapse into these diverse kingdoms? Yes. The nations of modern Europe descended from them.

This beast has ten horns but only seven heads. How could this be? History explains. When the church took over the western empire, three tribes—the Heruli, the Vandals, and the Ostrogoths—rejected the popular Christian teachings and authority. So Emperor Justinian went to war on behalf of Christianity. The last of the rebels, the Ostrogoths, fell in the year 538. Ten kingdoms. And three of them fell. Just a coincidence? Or striking fulfillment of prophecy? Which?

Now what about the other attributes of antichrist? Let's read Revelation 13, beginning with verse 5: "He was given a mouth speaking great things and blasphemies, and he was given authority to continue for forty-two months. Then he opened his mouth in blasphemy against God, to blaspheme His name, His tabernacle, and those who dwell in heaven. And it was granted to him to make war with the saints and to overcome them." Verses 5-7.

Everything fits together so far. But what about these forty-two months? What time period do they represent? With thirty days to a lunar month, forty-two months would be 1260 days.

Are these literal or symbolic days? Remember, we are dealing with symbols here. Short-lived beasts symbolize centuries of government. So a much longer time span than 1260 literal days is called for.

Our perplexity vanishes when we understand that in symbolic prophecy, a day represents a year. Ezekiel 4:6 is one of several scriptures explaining the year/day principle. The Reformers suggested these 1260 days represent 1260 years of medieval Christian church-and-state authority, and history confirms it. After the Ostrogoths were defeated in 538, the church and state held power for this prophetic period, 1260 years, ending in 1798.

Long centuries of turmoil had finally come to an end. But now we want to know, What is next for Christianity? We'll find out in our next chapter, "Bloodstained Stars and Stripes." Here, however, is a one-paragraph preview.

We learned in this chapter that an unfortunate union of church and state took place in the early and middle centuries. This coalition, so clearly predicted in Scripture, played havoc with humanity's God-given freedom. But now Revelation reveals that an image, a likeness, a similar union will appear again down here in the end time of our world's history. It will be a union of many Christian groups uniting with the state, again acting out the character of antichrist in an attempt to coerce your conscience and mine.

Meanwhile, let's thank God for preserving His people through the ages. Although challenged by apostasy, many church fathers remained outstanding Christians. Like Augustine, a bishop in north Africa four centuries after Christ. His writings blessed God's people for centuries to come.

As a young man, Augustine had wandered from the faith of his childhood. But his dear mother never lost hope. Kneeling with an open Bible, she pleaded God's promises as only a mother can. Drawn at last through those faithful prayers, Augustine almost yielded to the Holy Spirit. Almost, but not quite. He begged the Lord, "Give me purity—but not yet." Have you ever prayed like that?

Finally he surrendered fully to the Lord Jesus Christ. Then he could pen that famous prayer so dear to Christians everywhere, "You have made us for Yourself, and our hearts will not find rest until they rest in You."

O friend, never forget. God made you for Himself. Your heart will never find rest until you rest yourself in Jesus. And you can do that right now.

Bloodstained Stars and Stripes

America is being born again! We've repented of the psyche-delic sixties and the secular seventies. Like reformed prodigals heading home, we're turning back to God.

Religion is even revolutionizing government. Lobbyists scurry about the halls of Congress with Bibles under their arms. One predicts, "If Christians unite, we can pass any law or any amendment. And that's exactly what we intend to do!"

Revival by legislation. What happens when faith is enforced by law? Will it lead to bloodstained Stars and Stripes?

Did you know that America's first settlers, Protestants and Catholics alike, suffered religious persecution? And, believe it or not, prophecy predicts intolerance will arise again in this fair land of ours. And sooner than we may think!

We come now to the seventh chapter in our study of the prophecies of Revelation. Here we will explore the mark of the beast. We will discover how God's enemy will replace religious zeal with incredible deceptions. And anyone who refuses to be deceived by his mysterious image will be persecuted.

We Americans prize our freedoms. It's easy to forget that liberty did not come naturally. Our early settlers fled their English homeland to escape persecution. Yet they often failed to open their own arms to other religious refugees.

When William Penn's band of Quakers sailed past the colony of Massachusetts, they nearly fell prey to a seventeenth-century inquisition. Listen to this order from Cotton Mather, the famous Puritan clergyman:

59

"There be now at sea a ship called 'Welcome,' which has on board 100 or more of the heretics and malignants called Quakers.... The General Court has given sacred orders to ... waylay the said 'Welcome' ... and make captive the said Penn and his ungodly crew, so that the Lord may be glorified and not mocked with the heathen worship of these people.... We shall not only do the Lord great good by punishing the wicked, but we shall make great good for His minister and people. Yours in the bowels of Christ, Cotton Mather."

Can you believe it! Thank God, the preacher's persecuting pirates failed. Penn's Quakers landed safely, and with their quiet faith to encourage them, they settled our great state of Pennsylvania.

The Puritans not only tyrannized others, they oppressed their own citizens. They arrested a sea captain and locked him in the stocks after he was caught kissing his wife on Sunday. One poor man fell into a pond and skipped Sunday services to dry his suit. They whipped him in the name of Jesus. John Lewis and Sarah Chapman, two lovers, were brought to justice for "sitting together on the Lord's day under an apple tree in Goodman Chapman's orchard."

Incredible legalism! And this in a land of freedom?

The Puritans with their Sunday laws tragically missed the meaning of Sabbath rest. They enforced a Sabbath of works on the first day of the week instead of the biblical seventh-day Sabbath. Understanding the freedom of Sabbath rest would have safeguarded the Puritans from persecuting—from forcing religion upon others.

Throughout Christian history, ignorance of Sabbath rest has invariably sparked persecution. The Pharisees plotted to destroy Jesus after a dispute about the Sabbath. See Mark 3:1-6. The rigid religion of that day led them to crucify the Lord of the Sabbath.

Overcome by legalism, the early Christian church finally abandoned the Sabbath. Sunday, a pagan day, displaced the seventh day. And those refusing to reverence this day of the sun were persecuted. The record of history is open for all to read.

Now come with me down to the Reformation of the sixteenth century. Earnest men of God called the church back to the Bible alone and salvation by faith alone. But many Protestants retained many of their medieval traditions. Like the Puritans, for example, with their Sunday laws. When Roger Williams arrived in Massachusetts in 1631, he protested their legislated legalism. Williams claimed civil magistrates had no right to enforce personal religion.

The colony condemned him in 1635. He escaped arrest and fled into the snowy forest, finding refuge with the Indians. He later commented, "I would rather live with Christian savages, than with savage Christians."

Roger Williams bought land from the Indians and established a new colony dedicated to religious liberty. He called his settlement Providence, today the capital of Rhode Island. Williams welcomed Jews, Catholics, and Quakers as citizens in full and regular standing.

Nobody suffered for their faith—or for refusing to believe. Sad to say, later leaders of Rhode Island lapsed into legalism and intolerance. And sure enough, they passed a Sunday law in 1679, requiring certain acts on Sunday and forbidding others.

Some of those early American Sunday laws packed a real sting. A Virginia law of 1610 provided that "those who violated the Sabbath or failed to attend church services, morning and afternoon, should on the first offense lose their provisions and allowance of the whole week following; for the second, lose their allowance and be publicly whipped; and for the third, suffer death."

Death for Sunday breaking! Keep that old Virginia law in mind when you hear it said that Sunday laws are a part of the great American heritage—and we must return to the "faith of our fathers."

While still a boy in Virginia, James Madison heard a fearless Baptist minister preaching from the window of his prison cell. That day Madison dedicated his life to fight for freedom of conscience. Tirelessly he toiled with Thomas Jefferson and others to secure the First Amendment in our Bill of Rights. It reads simply and majestically: "Congress shall make no law respecting an establishment of religion, or prohibiting the free exercise thereof." Government, you see, must protect religion—but not promote it.

Our founding fathers knew well the dangers of trying to cure unbelief by reverting to force. And so does God. Jesus put it plainly: "Render therefore to Caesar the things that are Caesar's, and to God the things that are God's." Matthew 22:21. Religious laws and civil laws then and now must be kept separate, or intolerance rears its ugly head.

Take, for example, this much-discussed matter of school prayer—a very live but delicate issue. I believe our children should lift their hearts in prayer everywhere, including in school. Especially in school! But who should teach our kids to pray? Do we want Protestant prayers? Catholic prayers? Jewish prayers? Does it matter? Not long ago the California state legislature selected a Buddhist chaplain. Would you like Buddhist prayers in your local school?

Who gets to choose what to pray? And who gets left out? Are you beginning to see the problems here?

Some say restoring prayer in our schools will solve our educational problems. I certainly believe in the power of prayer, but that may be going too far. I remind you that all these years prayer has opened every session of Congress. Has the opening legislative prayer balanced the national budget? Has it solved Capitol Hill's many problems?

Maybe legislated prayer isn't such a cure-all after all. And besides, could enforcing school prayer, as innocent and commendable as it seems, lead to other intrusions into private religion? Perhaps even intolerance again? It has happened before.

Long ago, God's Word predicted the religious freedom we enjoy in the United States. But prophecy also warns that we will lose that liberty. We read about it in Revelation 13:11: "I saw another beast coming up out of the earth, and he had two horns like a lamb and spoke like a dragon."

What is happening here? Remember that a beast in symbolic Bible prophecy represents a power—a kingdom—a nation. So after the dark ages of persecution another power emerges, fresh from the earth. Remember also that in our first chapter we identified this new nation as the United States.

In the Old World, church and state had formed a unit. But here we have a new form of government with two lamblike horns—the peaceful *separation* of the two powers of government and religion.

According to the prediction, evidently our lamblike nation will reverse its gentle manners and behave like a dragon. We'll go back to the Old World ways of the Puritans. Unfortunately, some unusual and distressing events will soon occur in America. Let's see verses 12-14:

"He exercises all the authority of the first beast in his presence, and causes the earth and those who dwell in it to worship the first beast, whose deadly wound was healed. He performs great signs, so that he even makes fire come down from heaven on the earth in the sight of men. And he deceives those who dwell on the earth by those signs which he was granted to do in the sight of the beast, telling those who dwell on the earth to make an image to the beast who was wounded by the sword and lived."

By miracles, counterfeit miracles, our nation will lead the world to form an image to the Old World beast. What could this mean? An image is a copy of the original. The Old World beast was a union of church and state, a religious system wedded to government and supported by law. This New World image to the beast, being a copy of this system, must also be a religious system united to government and supported by national law. How did the original beast gain power? Knowing this, we can understand the present-day image to the beast.

Back in the year 321, Emperor Constantine declared Sunday a national day of worship. That was the first recorded Sunday law. Eventually Christianity became the official state religion by order of Emperor Theodosius. And soon this all-powerful church-and-state combination of the Middle Ages began persecuting all who resisted its teachings.

I ask you, Is there any such religious movement today in America? Are we moving toward a marriage of church and state?

Americans are fed up. Fed up with the permissiveness and immorality of the sixties. Even yesterday's flower children have learned respect for law and order. Americans have also grown tired of the godless humanism of the seventies. We don't want atheistic concepts taught to our children. We want our public schools to promote prayer.

Now believe me, I fervently agree with these important moral reforms. But has the pendulum swung too far? Many believe that as long as government doesn't favor one particular church, all is well. To them, separation of church and state means there's no state-sponsored denomination. This sounds good. And it has been tried before here in America.

The colony of Maryland was founded primarily as a refuge for persecuted Catholics, but Christians of all faiths were welcomed. The Maryland assembly in 1649 proclaimed an Act of Toleration, which provided that all who confess Jesus shall be welcomed and tolerated.

Yet even this so-called Act of Toleration, as sincere as it was, inspired religious persecution. No liberty whatever was provided for non-Christians. And all who chose to disbelieve a particular doctrine of the Trinity were declared to be under the death penalty.

Persecution. It naturally results when faith becomes law.

Remember the march on Washington? Washington for Jesus? I was invited by the leader of nineteen respected television ministers—some of them personal friends—to join that march. But I had to decline. Why? There was so much about it that was good and commendable and desperately needed. Asking a nation to pray! What is wrong with that?

Very, very commendable, I say. But notice, it was not a march on Pittsburgh or a march on Los Angeles. It was a march on Washington. And it was to be held on the capitol steps between the houses of our law-making bodies, with some of these lawmakers present to give legislative backing.

I couldn't believe that Jesus, in whose honor the march was held, would be demonstrating if He were here. The government in His day was desperately corrupt and in need of reform. Yet He made no attempt to correct the evils that were so obvious.

Remember, He didn't reform that way. He never led a protest march. He was not a political activist. Rather, He knew that the problem lay deep in the hearts of mankind.

Did Jesus commission us, "Go, coerce all men"? Or "Go and teach"? Did He tell us to "tarry in Washington, until you get support from the government"? Did He say, "Ye shall receive power, after ye have gained control of the legislature"? Does Christ want us to depend upon His power, or on government?

Certainly I wish everybody would believe in God and live according to biblical morality. That's what "It Is Written" is all about. I have given my life for such convictions. We *ought* to be concerned and speak out candidly when we see our large cities guilty of the same sins that brought judgment upon ancient Sodom. But it is God who decided the fate of Sodom. I don't think we have been authorized to play God!

It would be a wonderful thing, I say, if everyone lived according to the Bible. But whose interpretation of the Bible? That is the question. You can see why I've always opposed any attempt to legislate personal morality. It has never worked. It didn't work with the Puritans, and it won't work now.

Never forget it, friend. Religious legislation is legalism. National salvation by works. Enforcing religion on weak human nature may produce the appearance of correct living. Outward conduct may be changed. But not the heart. No wonder Jesus said, "If you love me, keep my commandments." Speak out against the evils, yes—but attempt to legislate, no. Since God never forces faith, why should we?

Do you see now why the Bible offers a different solution for the spiritual problems of our land—the seventh-day Sabbath rest? Week by week the Sabbath invites our personal expression of faith—faith in God as our Creator and faith in God as our Redeemer. Had the Sabbath always been kept, there would be no atheism. No godless societies. Sincere Sabbath rest makes us moral without becoming legalistic. The other commandments put us to work. Only the Sabbath offers us rest in Christ. It provides a foundation of faith for the duties to God and neighbor outlined in the other nine commandments.

But many who don't understand Sabbath rest want to bring

back Sunday legislation to our modern society. They are urging Sunday laws in the name of social welfare. Requiring one day off is good for society, they say. Good for the family. Even good for saving energy. But don't believe it! Despite good intentions, Sunday laws have always brought persecution.

And the Revelation says that history will repeat itself. Is the image to the beast being formed now? Zealous Christians already want to enforce the morality of the majority. What will happen next? Let's go back to Revelation 13. Look at verses 16 and 17. We're reading here about the image to the beast in America.

"He causes all, both small and great, rich and poor, free and slave, to receive a mark on their right hand or on their foreheads, and that no one may buy or sell except one who has the mark or the name of the beast, or the number of his name."

Here we have an international boycott resulting in the mark of the beast, enforced by the image to the beast. Before we explore some clues as to what the mark might be, remember God's seal, His memorial of creation? Understanding God's seal helps us identify the contrasting mark.

In warning us to avoid that mark, the Bible commands us to worship Him who made heaven and earth. See Revelation 14:6, 7. So God's creatorship is a key issue in the final conflict. What memorial of creation has He given us? Could it be that God will use Sabbath rest to measure the loyalty of everyone who chooses to worship Him? I'm simply asking questions.

If Sabbath rest in Jesus represents God's seal, can we see what the mark might be? The Bible says, "They have no rest day or night, who worship the beast and his image." Revelation 14:11. No rest—no Sabbath rest!

Now I know the matter of God's day of rest may seem trivial. But really, the Sabbath controversy isn't between one day or another. Remember when former Soviet leader Khrushchev visited America? When he took off his shoe and pounded it on the speaker's platform? Suppose he had demanded that we Americans abandon our Fourth of July holiday and celebrate Independence Day on the fifth of July instead? Would Khrushchev have had the right to change our day? And suppose we had accepted his new day? What would that say about our loyalty to America?

The Sabbath controversy, I say, isn't over a day at all. It's over leadership. Will we obey our God—or yield to another god? Whom will we trust? Where is our loyalty? The worldwide test is coming soon.

No one has the mark of the beast today. Let me repeat that statement. No one has the mark of the beast today. God will not permit anyone to receive that mark until the issues are out in the open. But when the issues are fully explained, and all have had opportunity to understand and see the critical and final nature of the matter—then, if we deliberately choose to obey a command of men in place of a command of God, if we yield to coercion and take the easy way out—we will have marked ourselves, by our actions, as no longer loyal to God.

It's difficult to see how Bible believers could ever turn to force and coercion. But then, we must remember the Puritans.

Who knows what would happen to our freedom if we faced a national crisis? History reveals that people would willingly exchange their liberties for personal security. Is it possible that the majority will exchange some of their freedoms for the sake of economic and military security in an emergency?

The safety zone between church and state has been shrinking. The pendulum has swung so far to the right that we hear increasing talk of legislating morality. One Protestant leader recently declared on the CBS Evening News that "this notion of the separation of church and state was the figment of some infidel's imagination." Imagine!

More and more, in harmony with Revelation 13, we see attempts to erode our freedoms. And whenever the power of the state has enforced the goals of the church, personal liberty has been forfeited. Persecution has followed. Remember those old American Sunday laws?

Now I feel sure of this—when liberty is lost in this country it won't be because Americans have suddenly become cruel and bigoted. Rather, I'm convinced that our freedoms will be voted away, legislated away, amended away by well-meaning Christians who do not realize what they are doing. They will sacrifice our liberties in an attempt to solve our national problems, in a backlash against decades of permissiveness. In a reaction against shrinking morality, in the belief that a return to lost values is our only hope of regaining God's favor—they will discover too late that they have forged shackles for the soul.

Racing toward the crisis hour, we cannot ignore or escape the issues at stake. And our decision must be our own. Satan would like to force his way in. Sometimes even loved ones want to enter—loved ones who do not understand. But God Himself won't violate our freedom to choose. He stands at the door of our hearts and knocks. He waits for us to accept His love. Even though it may cost us our lives.

I think of that winter night when the Roman legion was encamped by a lake in Armenia. Several versions of the story exist. But evidently forty soldiers had refused to recant their faith. And they were sentenced to die out on the frozen lake. Banded together in the numbing cold, they began to sing. The stern, pagan commander, on watch from his comfortable tent, heard the words: "Forty wrestlers, wrestling for Thee, O Christ. Claim for Thee the victory and ask from Thee the crown."

Strangely moved, that hardened general, so used to cursing and frantic pleas for mercy, listened intently. These were men of his own company, men who had angered the authorities by their faith. These were his forty heroes, distinguished soldiers. Must they die?

He moved out into the cold, gathered driftwood from the shore, and built a huge fire with flames leaping high into the night. Perhaps this would lead them to renounce their faith and save themselves. But no. Again the sound of the refrain met his ears, weaker now: "Forty wrestlers, wrestling for Thee, O Christ."

Then suddenly, the song changed: "Thirty-nine wrestlers, wrestling for Thee, O Christ—"

And all at once, as the song still floated in across the ice, one of the prisoners climbed up the bank and dropped by the fire, a shivering mass. The song of the forty was no more. One of the heroes had disavowed his faith.

On the shore, clearly outlined against the fire, stood the commander. Strange thoughts surged in his heart. Suddenly he took one brief look at the pitiful traitor before him and threw off his cloak. Before his soldiers could stop him, he raced down the bank and across the ice to the freezing men, casting back the words, "As I live, I'll have your place."

In a few moments the song, with a fresh note of triumph, was wafted again to the soldiers who had gathered, fearful and awe-struck, on the silent shore: "Forty wrestlers, wrestling for Thee, O Christ, Claim for Thee the victory and ask from Thee the crown!"

God help us to awake—to see the vital issues at stake—and commit ourselves to the blessed Lord and Saviour Jesus Christ—quietly determined that we will be true to Him.

Airlift From Armageddon

Hiroshima, Japan. August 6, 1945. Morning dawned bright and clear with the promise of a beautiful day. Then suddenly at 8:16 it happened. And our world has never been the same.

"We have had our last chance," warned General Douglas MacArthur, several weeks after we dropped the bomb. "If we do not devise some greater and more equitable system [of settling international problems], Armageddon will be at our door."

Armageddon. The very word chills our spines. It's frightening! And it's almost upon us! But what really is Armageddon? Does anybody know?

If you consult popular religious paperbacks, you'll find some conflicting forecasts about Armageddon. You'll read about Russians pressing down from the north, Africans driving up from the south, Europeans and Americans swarming in from the west—and 200 million Chinese marching over from the east. All converging upon a battlefield in northern Israel. Does such a military nightmare lurk around the corner? Let's open the Bible and find out in the book of Revelation, chapter 16. This is the only place in all of God's Word where we read about Armageddon. Notice verses 14 and 16:

"They are the spirits of demons, performing signs, which go out to the kings of the earth and of the whole world, to gather them to the battle of that great day of God Almighty." "And they gathered them together to the place called in Hebrew, Armageddon."

So there will be an Armageddon. It's the final conflict of

earth's history, called "the battle of that great day of God Almighty." Apparently it's a global war, for the kings of the whole world are involved. And more than human forces will be fighting. The spiritual armies of God and Satan will clash in this battle. See Revelation 17:14.

Evidently Armageddon means much more than World War III. It represents an all-out showdown between God and His enemies—the climax of the great controversy between good and evil. The whole world will be involved in Armageddon—and heaven too!

Where will this battle be fought? Well, history offers no record of a place called Armageddon. But the Bible gives us some hints. Our text says the word *Armageddon* comes from the Hebrew language. Shall we turn to the Hebrew for the meaning of the word? We discover that it is a combination of *har,* which means mountain, and *mageddon,* which many connect with Megiddo. So the name Armegeddon can be understood as "mountain of Megiddo."

The mountain of Megiddo—here is a clue we can work with. Megiddo was a small but important fortress city of Old Testament times. It lay north of Jerusalem near the plain of Esdraelon. Once in Scripture this plain itself is called the plain of Megiddo. At first it might seem to be a logical location for warfare. But some problems make us pause and probe further.

First of all, the plain of Megiddo is rather small to host a global war. It's just two thirds the size of Lake Tahoe in northern California. Could you imagine the armies of the whole world, with millions of soldiers, in such crowded quarters? How would they all fit? And what about the armies of heaven? Remember also that Megiddo of Armageddon is neither a city nor a plain—it's a mountain. We must find a mountain of Megiddo. A mountain with some spiritual significance for the armies of heaven.

Visiting the site of ancient Megiddo, as I have done on a number of occasions, might help us understand Armageddon. We drive eastward from the Mediterranean port city of Haifa and follow the Carmel ridge. After passing the northeastern ridge of Carmel, we see the ruins of the ancient city. But also looming large over the landscape at Megiddo is Mount Carmel.

Maybe Mount Carmel solves our dilemma. Does it represent Mount Megiddo, the scene of Armageddon? Did something happen at Carmel that could help us understand Armageddon? Long ago Mount Carmel hosted a dramatic showdown between God and His enemies. The prophet Elijah summoned the nation to appear on the mountain. He challenged them to judge between Baal, the sun god, and the true God of heaven: "How long will you falter between two opinions? If the Lord is God, follow Him; but if Baal, then follow him." 1 Kings 18:21.

God won a great victory that day at Carmel. The nation declared allegiance to Him rather than to Baal. With one mighty voice they proclaimed, "The Lord, He is God! The Lord, He is God!" Verse 39. Following their vote of confidence in God and His government, they punished the false prophets who had led God's people astray.

So the call to Mount Carmel meant judgment—evaluating God and His government. And then a judgment of those who rejected Him. Should we expect some similar type of judgment in connection with Armageddon? What does the Bible say? Scripture reveals that Armageddon will occur during the seven plagues at the close of earth's history. Let's learn more about these plagues. God has been so patient all these years, sending sunshine and rain upon the good and evil alike. Now suddenly He sends wrath instead of rain. Why?

Let's go to Revelation 11. Has some type of judgment taken place in heaven? Has a verdict been reached? Let's read, beginning with verse 15: "Then the seventh angel sounded: And there were loud voices in heaven, saying, 'The kingdoms of this world have become the kingdoms of our Lord and of His Christ, and He shall reign forever and ever!' And the twenty-four elders who sat before God on their thrones fell on their faces and worshiped God, saying: 'We give You thanks, O Lord God Almighty, the One who is and who was and who is to come, because You have taken Your great power and reigned. The nations were angry, and Your wrath has come, and the time of the dead, that they should be judged, and that You should reward Your servants the prophets and the saints, and those who fear

Your name, small and great, and should destroy those who destroy the earth.' " Verses 15-18.

A remarkable scenario. What's happening here? A time to be judged, the text tells us. A judgment up in heaven while life continues here on earth. Just as at Carmel, God's government must be vindicated before He assumes His authority to punish the wicked. What's the purpose of this judgment? God cares about His reputation. He knows loyalty depends upon trust. So He determines to prove Himself trustworthy, allowing Himself to be audited. This same type of judgment occurs in the business world today. A corporation president, charged with dishonesty, may decide to open the books so every employee can see he has been just and fair. He wants to be trusted.

Now suppose he hasn't been honest in his dealings. Then he'll do everything possible to prevent such an audit. But God has nothing to hide. He invites inspection of His government. The apostle Paul understood this judgment when he wrote, "Let God be found true, though every man be found a liar, as it is written, 'That Thou mightest be justified in Thy words, and mightest prevail when Thou art judged.' " Romans 3:4, NASB.

So God will prevail when He is judged. Just as He won His case at Mount Carmel. God convinces His creation He is worthy of their worship. Satan's challenge is defeated at Armageddon. The kingdoms of this world become God's beyond dispute. Citizens of the universe stand behind Him as He rewards His people and punishes rebellion with the seven last plagues.

Is this judgment portrayed in the book of Revelation? Come with me to chapter 5. In Revelation 4 and 5, the apostle John describes what many consider to be the actual judgment scene in heaven's temple. Angels—myriads of them—gather to weigh the evidence. The evidence about God and His followers on earth. Scrolls, old-fashioned books, are opened.

Now, what's happening in the courts of heaven? Let's notice Revelation 5, verses 2, 3.

"I saw a strong angel proclaiming with a loud voice, 'Who is worthy to open the scroll and to loose its seals?' And no one in heaven or on the earth or under the earth was able to open the scroll, or to look at it."

Who is worthy? This is the crucial question. John watches with interest to see who will pass the judgment. But no one is worthy. No one in heaven. No one on the earth measures up to the scrutiny of judgment. Not even John himself, a disciple of Jesus. And no one under the earth—no one in the grave—is worthy.

John begins to "weep greatly." (NASB) Is this disappointed curiosity? No, much more than that. He's worried about the judgment. If nobody can survive the scrutiny of heaven's court, what hope does he have? Everyone is unworthy. Everyone, that is, but Jesus. See verse 5:

"One of the elders said to me, 'Do not weep. Behold, the Lion of the tribe of Judah, the Root of David, has prevailed to open the scroll and to loose its seven seals.' "

What comfort for our hearts—the Lord Jesus Christ is declared worthy! He prevails in heaven's court. And when our Saviour wins the verdict, we win too, for our lives belong to Him. We overcome in the blood of the Lamb.

Remember the story of those plagues in Egypt? What saved God's people from the death angel? Blood on their doorposts. God promised, "When I see the blood, I will pass over you; and the plague shall not be on you to destroy you when I strike the land of Egypt." Exodus 12:13.

The blood, friend—that's what counts! The blood of Jesus. We're safe from the plagues in our Saviour's blood. When every soul decides for life or death, earth's harvest will be ripe. All who trust in Jesus are sealed for eternal life. And those who refuse God's salvation will lose their lives.

You may remember hearing about Harry Truman. I don't mean the former president. This was the Harry Truman who owned the Mount Saint Helens Lodge in the state of Washington. Those who lived near the volcanic mountain had been warned about an imminent eruption. But some of them, including eighty-four-year-old Harry, refused all attempts to save them from their beloved mountain.

Harry told his would-be rescuers, "There's nothing that mountain could do to scare me off." Saint Helens, you see, was like a friend to him. He felt safe, having lived there for fifty-four years. He even boasted, "No one knows more about this mountain than Harry, and it don't dare blow up on him."

But it did. It happened the morning of May 18, 1980. An explosion twenty-five hundred times more powerful than the blast that ripped Hiroshima came as an overwhelming surprise. Today poor Harry and dozens of others lie buried beneath the volcanic mud. They gambled their lives with the mountain—and lost. They had been warned, but they refused to be saved. Why is it we find it so hard to heed warnings?

Just before the destruction of this world, God sends three angels with special urgent worldwide warnings. We find them in Revelation 14. Each angel proclaims a segment of the message that is God's last communication to the human race. Of course, these angels are symbolic. They are not flying over our heads with a megaphone. We find the first warning in Revelation 14:6, 7:

"I saw another angel flying in the midst of heaven, having the everlasting gospel to preach to those who dwell on the earth—to every nation, tribe, tongue, and people—saying with a loud voice, 'Fear God and give glory to Him, for the hour of His judgment has come; and worship Him who made heaven and earth, the sea and springs of water.' "

Here's the everlasting gospel, the grand old message of salvation. But now with a new urgency. Why? Because "the hour of His judgment has come." A judgment like that at Mount Carmel of long ago.

Next comes the second angel, warning about false worship. Then finally the third angel, sounding the alarm about the mark of the beast. So every soul decides for life and death. Those faithful to God receive His seal. The disobedient receive the mark of the beast and the plagues. After the seventh and last plague, Christ returns to airlift His people from Armageddon. We will rise through the sky to our heavenly home. And what a homecoming that will be!

Remember the day our hostages came home from Iran? The long ordeal ended almost as suddenly as it had begun. The fear and the hunger, the blindfolds and the isolation and the beatings, the terrible loneliness, the fake firing squads—all slipped into the past. Four hundred and forty-four dull, dragging, seemingly endless days suddenly gave way to a tumult of joy and reunion. A welcome that couldn't happen except in a dream. Yet it was happening—happening to fifty-two Americans who in their darkest hours had been tempted to think they had been forgotten.

It would take a while to sort it all out and be convinced that it was real! Telephones! Milk to drink! No blindfolds! Moving about without asking permission! German children singing to make up for the Christmases they had missed. The Statue of Liberty lighted for the first time since 1976! Kissing American soil! Church bells ringing! Falling at last into the arms of loved ones! The memories were theirs to keep.

And each day brought more pictures to hang in memory's hall. Pictures framed by bus windows as they inched through the cheering crowds. The Lincoln Memorial bathed in colored lights. The President praying simply, "Dear God, thank You! Thank You for what You've done!"

Americans had not been content simply to tie yellow ribbons 'round old oak trees. They tied them everywhere. On trees. On cars. On planes. On gates. On buildings. They tied one completely around the National Geographic Building. And the biggest yellow ribbon in history was tied in a bow around the Superdome in New Orleans!

Miles and miles of ribbons—beside the highways and above them. Corridors of welcome the freed hostages would never forget! Americans watched it all—from the streets and from their living rooms—and wept for joy. The hostages were safe! They were free! Home at last—and how happy we were to have them back!

What a celebration! Just like that unforgettable day in France at the end of World War I. As twenty thousand soldiers approached the Arc de Triomphe, a great choir sang the joyful challenge, "By what right do you come to the arch of victory?" Can you imagine the inspiration and emotion when 20,000 voices responded, "We come by the blood-red banner of Verdun!"

Soon the Lord Jesus Christ will sweep through the gates of

heaven with the redeemed of all the ages. I can imagine the angel choir greeting us with the challenge, "By what right do you enter here?" And we will unite in the mighty chorus, "We come by the blood-red banner of Calvary!" What a day that will be! Please don't miss it!

After the homecoming celebration, we will settle down to enjoy eternity with our Lord and Saviour. Listen to this description of our paradise home. It's taken from *The Great Controversy,* one of my favorite books.

"There are ever-flowing streams, clear as crystal, and beside them waving trees cast their shadows upon the paths prepared for the ransomed of the Lord. There the wide-spreading plains swell into hills of beauty, and the mountains of God rear their lofty summits. On those peaceful plains, beside those living streams, God's people, so long pilgrims and wanderers, shall find a home."

"The great controversy is ended. Sin and sinners are no more. The entire universe is clean. One pulse of harmony and gladness beats through the vast creation. From Him who created all, flow life and light and gladness, throughout the realms of illimitable space. From the minutest atom to the greatest world, all things, animate and inanimate, in their unshadowed beauty and perfect joy, declare that God is love."— Pages 675, 678.

O friend, can you picture it? All things new! Just as they were at creation. Won't it be wonderful when Jesus comes? And I believe He is coming soon! God help us to join with the apostle, responding, "Even so, come, Lord Jesus!"

And now as we close this series on Revelation, my prayer for you is found in the very last verse of the book: "The grace of our Lord be with you all. Amen." Revelation 22:21.

Dear Friend:

You have just finished reading this brief but important resumé of the fascinating book of Revelation. If you find a new concern developing, I earnestly hope you will proceed with further study of the Bible—especially the Revelation of Jesus, which reveals "the things which shall shortly come to pass." Several opportunities for continuing in-depth study of the Revelation are available to you.

First, you will find a description of two very helpful volumes on the inside back cover of this book—*God Cares,* volumes 1 and 2. Volume 1 explores the book of Daniel, and volume 2 is an explanation of Revelation. The books are scholarly but easy to read and understand. They will make deeper Bible study warm and appealing.

Second, Revelation Seminars are being conducted by "It Is Written" representatives in all areas of North America and in many countries overseas. Let me know of your interest, and I will do my best to acquaint you with the nearest seminar location.

And finally, I have recently completed thirty easy-to-understand video-cassette Bible studies. They are designed to cover the essential messages of Revelation as they relate to the entire Bible. The studies are entitled "Truth for the End Time." Just contact my office for further information on this series.

God bless you richly in your earnest search for truth. I am confident that you will not be disappointed as you study to know Him better, whom to know is life eternal—the Lord Jesus Christ, my Friend and your Friend.

Faithfully,
George E. Vandeman

It Is Written
Box 0,
Thousand Oaks, California 91360